Busy Ant Maths

2nd EDITION

Textbook 5

T0340535

Series editor and author: Peter Clarke

William Collins' dream of knowledge for all began with the publication of his first book in 1819.

A self-educated mill worker, he not only enriched millions of lives, but also founded a flourishing publishing house. Today, staying true to this spirit, Collins books are packed with inspiration, innovation and practical expertise.

They place you at the centre of a world of possibility and give you exactly what you need to explore it.

Collins. Freedom to teach.

Published by Collins

An imprint of HarperCollins*Publishers*
The News Building, 1 London Bridge Street, London,
SE1 9GF, UK

HarperCollins*Publishers*
Macken House, 39/40 Mayor Street Upper, Dublin 1,
D01 C9W8, Ireland

Browse the complete Collins catalogue at
collins.co.uk

© HarperCollins*Publishers* Limited 2023

10 9 8 7 6 5 4 3 2 1

ISBN 978-0-00-861376-1

All rights reserved. No part of this publication may be reproduced, stored in a retrieval system, or transmitted in any form by any means, electronic, mechanical, photocopying, recording or otherwise, without the prior written permission of the Publisher or a licence permitting restricted copying in the United Kingdom issued by the Copyright Licensing Agency Ltd, 5th Floor, Shackleton House, 4 Battle Bridge Lane, London SE1 2HX.

British Library Cataloguing-in-Publication Data

A catalogue record for this publication is available from the British Library.

Series editor: Peter Clarke
Author: Peter Clarke
Product manager: Holly Woolnough
Editorial assistant: Nalisha Vansia
Copy editor: Tanya Solomons
Proofreader: Catherine Dakin
Illustrator: Ann Paganuzzi
Cover designer: Amparo Barrera
Cover illustrator: Amparo Barrera
Internal designer: 2Hoots Publishing Services
Typesetter: David Jimenez
Production controller: Alhady Ali
Printed and bound in Great Britain by Martins the Printers

Busy Ant Maths 2nd edition components are compatible with the 1st edition of Busy Ant Maths.

This book is produced from independently certified FSC™ paper to ensure responsible forest management.

For more information visit: harpercollins.co.uk/green

Acknowledgements

p88bl Natalia Lisovskaya/Shutterstock; p88br Tarzhanova/Shutterstock.

Contents

Fractions

Decimals

Percentages

Year 5 Number facts

How to use this book

This book shows different pictures, models and images (representations) to explain important mathematical ideas to do with number.

At the start of each double page is a brief description of the key mathematical ideas.

The key words related to the mathematical ideas are shown in colour. It's important that you understand what each of these words mean.

The main part of each double page explains the mathematical ideas. It might include pictures, models or an example.

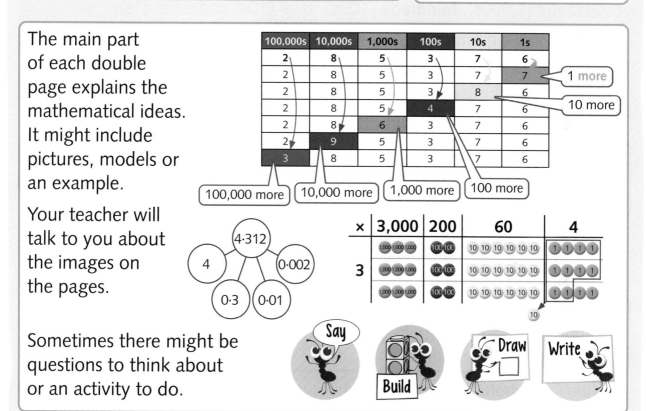

100,000s	10,000s	1,000s	100s	10s	1s
2	8	5	3	7	6
2	8	5	3	7	7	1 more
2	8	5	3	8	6	10 more
2	8	5	4	7	6
2	8	6	3	7	6
2	9	5	3	7	6
3	8	5	3	7	6

100,000 more   10,000 more   1,000 more   100 more

Your teacher will talk to you about the images on the pages.

Sometimes there might be questions to think about or an activity to do.

Say   Build   Draw   Write

Pages 6-7

This refers to mathematical ideas on other pages that you need to understand before learning about the ideas on these two pages.

Pages 24-29, 48-55

This refers to mathematical ideas on other pages that use or build upon the ideas on these two pages.

 This helps you think more deeply about the mathematical ideas.

 Hint   Use the pages in this book to help you answer the questions in the Pupil Books.

Numbers to 1,000,000

The position of each digit in a number tells us its value. Composing and decomposing numbers makes them easier to calculate.

5-digit numbers

5-digit numbers are made of **tens of thousands** (10,000s), thousands (1,000s), **hundreds** (100s), tens (10s) and ones (1s).

48,273 is a 5-digit number.

5-digit numbers have two thousands numbers – **tens of thousands** (10,000s) and thousands (1,000s).

48,273 is written as forty-eight thousand, two hundred and seventy-three.

The digit 4 is in the **tens of thousands** position. The **value** of the 4 is 4 **ten thousands** or **40,000**.

The digit 2 is in the **hundreds** position. The value of the 2 is 2 **hundreds** or **200**.

The digit 3 is in the ones position. The value of the 3 is 3 ones or 3.

10,000s	1,000s	100s	10s	1s
4	8	2	7	3

The digit 8 is in the thousands position. The value of the 8 is 8 thousands or 8,000.

The digit 7 is in the tens position. The value of the 7 is 7 tens or 70.

To find the **whole number**, we **add** the values together.

40,000 + 8,000 + 200 + 70 + 3 = 48,273

6-digit numbers

6-digit numbers are made of **hundreds of thousands** (100,000s), **tens of thousands** (10,000s), thousands (1,000s), **hundreds** (100s), tens (10s) and ones (1s).

284,369 is a 6-digit number.

48,273 has 48 **thousands**, 2 **hundreds**, 7 tens and 3 ones.

6-digit numbers have three thousands numbers – **hundreds of thousands** (100,000), **tens of thousands** (10,000) and thousands (1,000).

284,369 is written as two hundred and eighty-four thousand, three hundred and sixty-nine.

The digit 2 is in the **hundreds of thousands** position. The value of the 2 is 2 **hundred thousands** or **200,000**.

The digit 4 is in the thousands position. The value of the 4 is 4 thousands or 4,000.

The digit 6 is in the tens position. The value of the 6 is 6 tens or 60.

100,000s	10,000s	1,000s	100s	10s	1s
2	8	4	3	6	9

The digit 8 is in the **tens of thousands** position. The value of the 8 is 8 **ten thousands** or **80,000**.

The digit 3 is in the **hundreds** position. The value of the 3 is 3 **hundreds** or **300**.

The digit 9 is in the ones position. The value of the 9 is 9 ones or 9.

To find the whole number, we add the values together.

200,000 + 80,000 + 4,000 + 300 + 60 + 9 = 284,369

284,369 has 284 thousands, 3 **hundreds**, 6 tens and 9 ones.

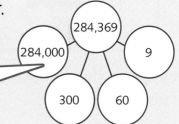

5- and 6-digit numbers can be written with a comma or a space separating the **hundreds** and the thousands.

48,273 and 284,369 or 48 273 and 284 369

Look at the Gattegno chart below. It shows ones, tens, **hundreds**, thousands, **tens of thousands** and **hundreds of thousands**.

What patterns do you notice? How are the rows the same? How are they different? What happens in each column of numbers?

Say

Point to numbers in different rows and say the number name.

100,000	200,000	300,000	400,000	500,000	600,000	700,000	800,000	900,000
10,000	20,000	30,000	40,000	50,000	60,000	70,000	80,000	90,000
1,000	2,000	3,000	4,000	5,000	6,000	7,000	8,000	9,000
100	200	300	400	500	600	700	800	900
10	20	30	40	50	60	70	80	90
1	2	3	4	5	6	7	8	9

Pages 8–45

Represent numbers to 1,000,000 in different ways
Pages 6-7

We can decompose numbers to show the place value of each digit. We can also decompose (or regroup) numbers in other ways.

 Remember We can **decompose** or **partition** 23,654 into **tens of thousands**, **thousands**, **hundreds**, **tens** and **ones**.

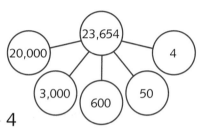

$$23,654 = 20,000 + 3,000 + 600 + 50 + 4$$

We can decompose or **regroup** 23,654 in other ways to help us with calculations.

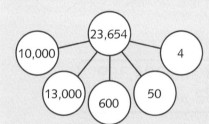

$$23,654 = 10,000 + 13,000 + 600 + 50 + 4$$

$$23,654 = 20,000 + 2,000 + 1,600 + 40 + 14$$

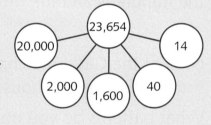

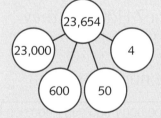

$$23,654 = 23,000 + 600 + 50 + 4$$

$$23,654 = 12,000 + 10,000 + 1,600 + 54$$

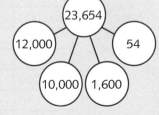

$$23,654 = 23,000 + 600 + 54$$

How else could you regroup 23,654?

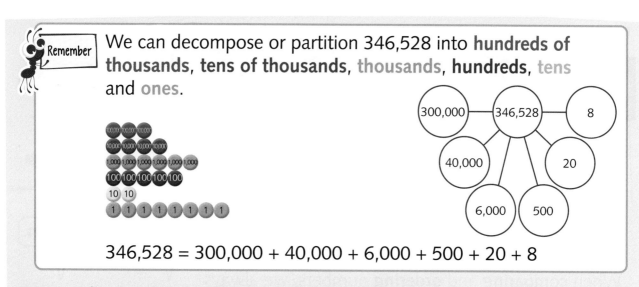

Remember We can decompose or partition 346,528 into **hundreds of thousands**, **tens of thousands**, thousands, **hundreds**, tens and ones.

$$346,528 = 300,000 + 40,000 + 6,000 + 500 + 20 + 8$$

We can decompose or regroup 346,528 in other ways.

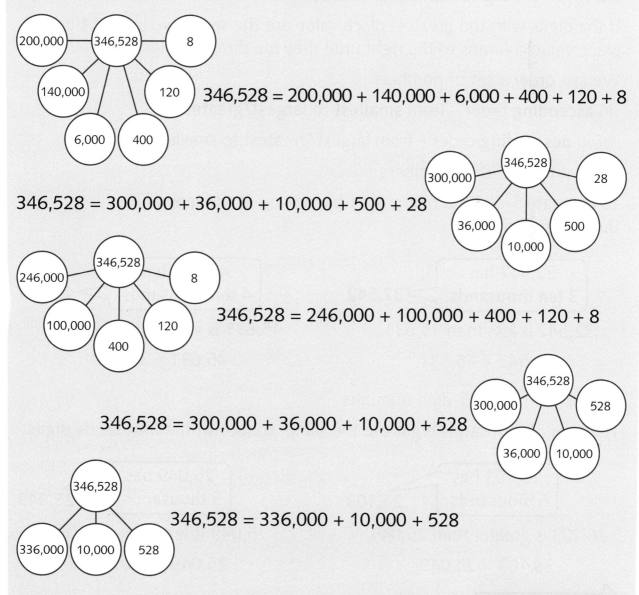

$$346,528 = 200,000 + 140,000 + 6,000 + 400 + 120 + 8$$

$$346,528 = 300,000 + 36,000 + 10,000 + 500 + 28$$

$$346,528 = 246,000 + 100,000 + 400 + 120 + 8$$

$$346,528 = 300,000 + 36,000 + 10,000 + 528$$

$$346,528 = 336,000 + 10,000 + 528$$

Can you think of other ways to regroup 346,528?

Pages 18-25, 30-45

Compare and order numbers to 1,000,000

Pages 6-7

When we compare and order numbers, we use language such as greater/greatest, smaller/smallest, and more than/less than. We can also use the inequality symbols > and < to compare and order numbers.

It's important to remember what these **inequality** symbols mean.

greater than   less than

When **comparing** and **ordering** numbers, we always start with the **digits** with the greatest **place value**.

>   <

If the digits with the greatest place value are the same, we look at the place value columns to the right until they are different digits.

We can **order** a set of numbers:

in **ascending** order – from **smallest** to **largest/greatest**

or in **descending** order – from largest/greatest to smallest.

Look at these 5-digit numbers.

To **compare** 5-digit numbers, start by looking at the **tens of thousands** digits.

> 32,542 has
> 3 ten thousands.   **32,542**

32,542 is less than 45,631.

32,542 < 45,631

> 45,631 has
> 4 ten thousands.   **45,631**

45,631 is greater than 32,542.

45,631 > 32,542

Now look at these 5-digit numbers.

The **tens of thousands** digits are the same, so look at the thousands digits.

> 26,103 has
> 6 thousands.   **26,103**

26,103 is greater than 25,049.

26,103 > 25,049

> 25,049 has
> 5 thousands.   **25,049**

25,049 is less than 26,103.

25,049 < 26,103

We use the same method when ordering numbers.

Look at these numbers.

| 10,453 | | 10,318 | | 10,497 | | 10,632 | | 10,405 |

If the **tens of thousands** and thousands digits are the same, then look at the **hundreds** digits.

If the **tens of thousands**, thousands and **hundreds** digits are the same, then look at the tens digits.

If the **tens of thousands**, thousands, **hundreds** and tens digits are the same, then look at the ones digits.

We can use a number line to help us order numbers.

So, in ascending order, the above numbers are:

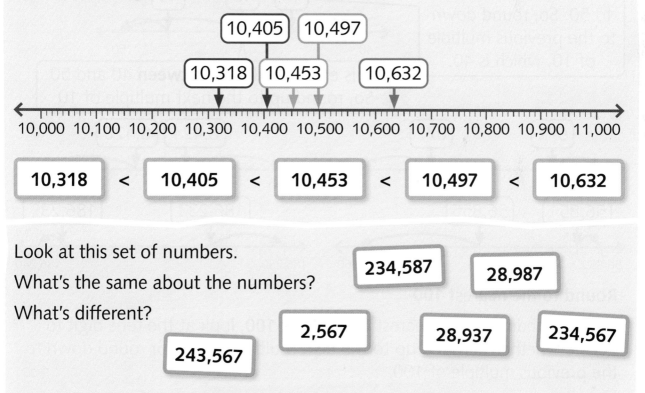

| 10,318 | < | 10,405 | < | 10,453 | < | 10,497 | < | 10,632 |

Look at this set of numbers.

What's the same about the numbers?

What's different?

| 234,587 | | 28,987 |

| 2,567 | | 28,937 | | 234,567 |

| 243,567 |

When comparing and ordering numbers with the same number of digits, if the digits with the greatest place value are all the same, what do you look at next?

What's different about comparing and ordering numbers with the same number of digits and comparing and ordering numbers with different numbers of digits?

Order the set of numbers above in descending order.

Pages 68-69

Round numbers to 1,000,000

Pages 6-7

Rounding changes a number to another number that is close to it in value. It makes the number easier to use and is useful when estimating.

Round to the nearest 10

When **rounding** numbers to the nearest **multiple of 10**, look at the ones digit to decide whether to **round up** to the **next** multiple of 10 or **round down** to the **previous** multiple of 10.

We can round 2-, 3-, 4-, 5- and 6-digit numbers to the nearest 10.

48 is closer to 50 than to 40. So, round up to the next multiple of 10, which is 50.

43 is closer to 40 than to 50. So, round down to the previous multiple of 10, which is 40.

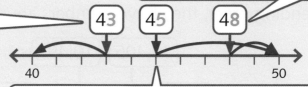

45 is exactly **halfway between** 40 and 50. So, round up to the next multiple of 10.

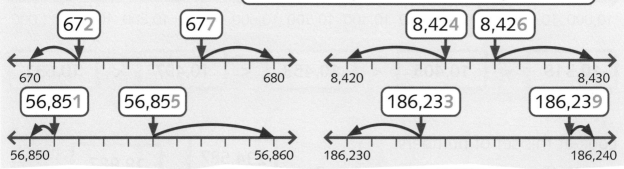

Round to the nearest 100

When rounding to the nearest **multiple of 100**, look at the tens digit to decide whether to round up to the next multiple of 100 or round down to the previous multiple of 100.

We can round 3-, 4-, 5- and 6-digit numbers to the nearest 100.

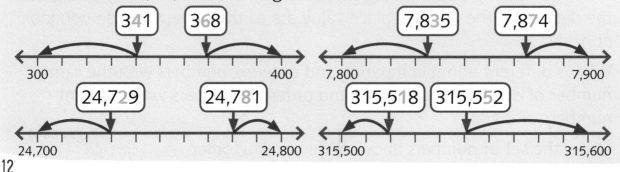

Round to the nearest 1,000

When rounding to the nearest **multiple of 1,000**, look at the **hundreds** digit to decide whether to round up to the next multiple of 1,000 or round down to the previous multiple of 1,000.

We can round 4-, 5- and 6-digit numbers to the nearest 1,000.

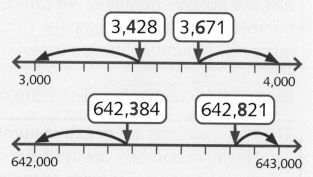

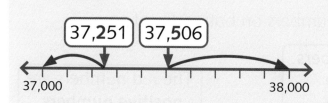

Round to the nearest 10,000

When rounding to the nearest **multiple of 10,000**, look at the thousands digit to decide whether to round up to the next multiple of 10,000 or round down to the previous multiple of 10,000.

We can round 5- and 6-digit numbers to the nearest 10,000.

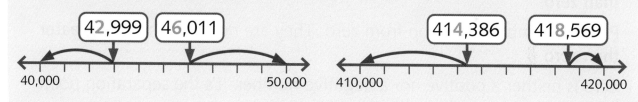

Round to the nearest 100,000

When rounding to the nearest **multiple of 100,000**, look at the **tens of thousands** digit to decide whether to round up to the next multiple of 100,000 or round down to the previous multiple of 100,000.

We can round 6-digit numbers to the nearest 100,000.

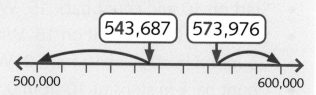

 Write three different 6-digit numbers.

Write

Round each of your numbers to the nearest 10, 100, 1,000, 10,000 and 100,000.

Pages 20-23, 36-45 70-71

Negative numbers

Just like positive numbers, we can count on and back in negative numbers. We can also compare, order and estimate negative numbers. A number line is a useful tool to help us with this.

Look at this number line. There are numbers on both sides of **zero**.

The blue numbers are **negative numbers**. Negative numbers always have a negative sign (–) in front of them.

The red numbers are **positive numbers**.

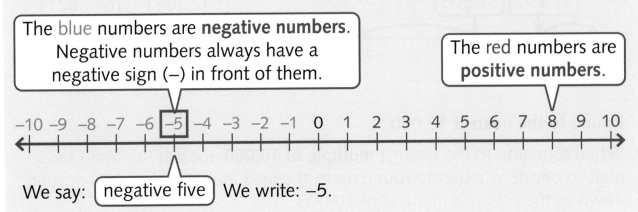

We say: negative five We write: –5.

Negative numbers count back from zero. They are numbers that are **less than zero**.

Positive numbers count on from zero. They are numbers that are **greater than zero**.

Zero is neither a positive nor a negative number. It's the separation point between positive and negative numbers.

 Say Look at this number line.

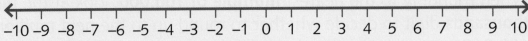

- Start on 10 and count back 15. What number do you land on?
- Start on –10 and count on 18. What number do you land on?
- Count on in steps of 10 from 0. What is the 7th step?
- Count back in steps of 10 from 0. What must the 7th step be?
- Count on in steps of 2 from 0. What is the 9th step?
- Count back in steps of 2 from 0. What must the 9th step be?
- Count on in steps of 5 from 0. What is the 8th step?
- Count back in steps of 5 from 0. What must the 8th step be?

A **number sequence** is a **pattern** of numbers that follows a **rule**.

A rule involves adding, subtracting, multiplying or dividing the previous number in the sequence.

The numbers in a sequence are called **terms**.

Look at these number lines. They show different number sequences.

Count back in 5s from 14.

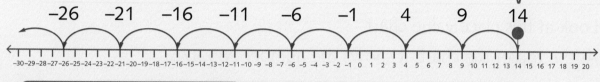

Count on in 4s from −20.

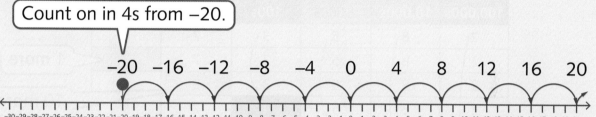

Count back in 6s from 17.

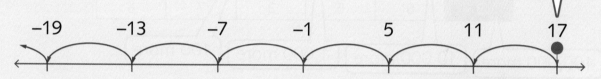

Look at this number sequence:

45, 36, 27, 18, 9, 0, −9, −18, …

The rule is 'Start on 45, subtract 9.'

What are the next three terms in this sequence?

Order the sets of numbers by estimating where each number will be on the number line.

6   −14   −5   12

−37   26   35   −24

Count in 1s, 10s, 100s, 1,000s, 10,000s and 100,000s

Pages 6-7

Being able to count forwards and backwards in steps of 1, 10, 100, 1,000, 10,000 and 100,000 helps us to develop a deeper understanding of place value and is useful when calculating.

Look at this place value chart.

At the top of the chart, it shows the number 285,376.

100,000s	10,000s	1,000s	100s	10s	1s	
2	8	5	3	7	6	
2	8	5	3	7	7	**1 more**
2	8	5	3	8	6	
2	8	5	4	7	6	10 more
2	8	6	3	7	6	
2	9	5	3	7	6	
3	8	5	3	7	6	

100,000 more   10,000 more   1,000 more   100 more

Say What is 1, 10, 100, 1,000, 10,000 and 100,000 **less than** 285,376?

How can you use a Gattegno chart to find 1, 10, 100, 1,000, 10,000 and 100,000 more or less than 285,376?

100,000	200,000	300,000	400,000	500,000	600,000	700,000	800,000	900,000
10,000	20,000	30,000	40,000	50,000	60,000	70,000	80,000	90,000
1,000	2,000	3,000	4,000	5,000	6,000	7,000	8,000	9,000
100	200	300	400	500	600	700	800	900
10	20	30	40	50	60	70	80	90
1	2	3	4	5	6	7	8	9

What patterns do you notice when you add or subtract 1, 10, 100, 1,000, 10,000 or 100,000?

What is the same and what is different about finding 1, 10, 100, 1,000, 10,000 and 100,000 more or less on a place value chart and a Gattegno chart?

A **number sequence** is a **pattern** of numbers that follows a **rule**.

A rule involves adding, subtracting, multiplying or dividing the previous number in the sequence.

The numbers in a sequence are called **terms**.

Remember

Look at these number lines. They each show a different number sequence.

What are the next three numbers in each sequence?

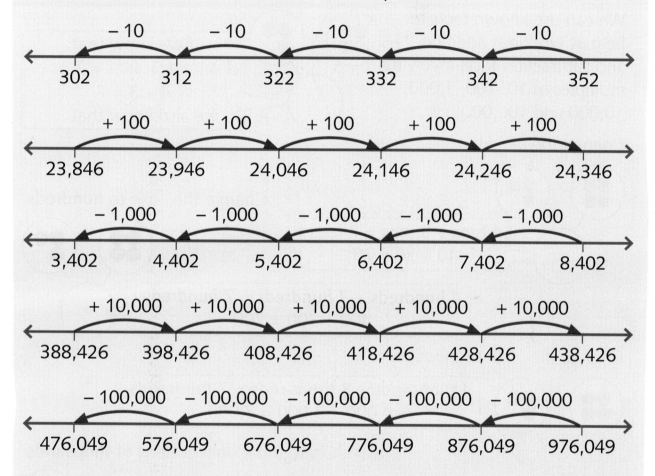

| − 10 | − 10 | − 10 | − 10 | − 10 |
| 302 | 312 | 322 | 332 | 342 | 352 |

| + 100 | + 100 | + 100 | + 100 | + 100 |
| 23,846 | 23,946 | 24,046 | 24,146 | 24,246 | 24,346 |

| − 1,000 | − 1,000 | − 1,000 | − 1,000 | − 1,000 |
| 3,402 | 4,402 | 5,402 | 6,402 | 7,402 | 8,402 |

| + 10,000 | + 10,000 | + 10,000 | + 10,000 | + 10,000 |
| 388,426 | 398,426 | 408,426 | 418,426 | 428,426 | 438,426 |

| − 100,000 | − 100,000 | − 100,000 | − 100,000 | − 100,000 |
| 476,049 | 576,049 | 676,049 | 776,049 | 876,049 | 976,049 |

Use a place value chart or the Gattegno chart to find the missing terms in each of these sequences. You will need to identify the rule first.

5,467	5,367	5,267			
867	877	887			
250,048	350,048		550,048		
	56,967	46,967			16,967
		370,982	371,982		373,982

Pages 18-23

Use known addition and subtraction facts

Pages 6–9, 16–17

Being able to recall the addition and subtraction facts to 20 helps us to add and subtract multiples of 10, 100, 1,000, 10,000 and 100,000.

We can use known facts to help us work out addition and subtraction facts involving multiples of 10, 100, 1,000, 10,000 and 100,000.

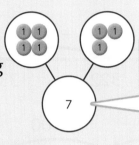

If we know that:
4 ones + 3 ones = 7 ones
4 + 3 = 7
we also know that …

Change the ones to tens.

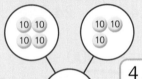

4 tens + 3 tens = 7 tens
40 + 30 = 70

Change the ones to hundreds.

4 hundreds + 3 hundreds = 7 hundreds
400 + 300 = 700

Change the ones to thousands.

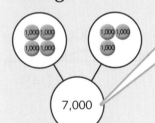

4 thousands + 3 thousands = 7 thousands
4,000 + 3,000 = 7,000

Change the ones to tens of thousands.

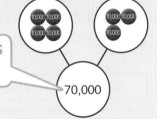

40 thousands + 30 thousands = 70 thousands
40,000 + 30,000 = 70,000

Change the ones to hundreds of thousands.

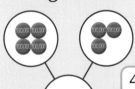

400 thousands + 300 thousands = 700 thousands
400,000 + 300,000 = 700,000

Addition can be done in any order – it's **commutative**.

Addition and subtraction are related. If we know one addition or subtraction fact, we know three other related facts (**fact families**).

So,

4 + 3 = 7
3 + 4 = 7
7 − 3 = 4
7 − 4 = 3

and

40 + 30 = 70
30 + 40 = 70
70 − 30 = 40
70 − 40 = 30

and

400 + 300 = 700
300 + 400 = 700
700 − 300 = 400
700 − 400 = 300

and

4,000 + 3,000 = 7,000
3,000 + 4,000 = 7,000
7,000 − 3,000 = 4,000
7,000 − 4,000 = 3,000

and

40,000 + 30,000 = 70,000
30,000 + 40,000 = 70,000
70,000 − 30,000 = 40,000
70,000 − 40,000 = 30,000

and

400,000 + 300,000 = 700,000
300,000 + 400,000 = 700,000
700,000 − 300,000 = 400,000
700,000 − 400,000 = 300,000

Say If you know that 17,000 − 5,000 = 12,000, what other addition and subtraction facts do you know?

  Write Work out these calculations. Show all the steps in your thinking. Think carefully about which mental strategies you are going to use. **Say**

6,473 + 999 = ☐

7,548 − 990 = ☐

18,000 + 28,000 = ☐

32,000 − 630 = ☐

268,000 + 45,000 = ☐

300,000 − 17,000 = ☐

160,000 + 160,000 = ☐

506,000 − 199,000 = ☐

280,000 + 500,000 = ☐

825,000 − 401,000 = ☐

Compare your answers with a partner, and talk about the strategies you used.

Which strategies were the most effective and efficient?

Pages 20-23, 72-75

19

Add whole numbers with more than 4 digits

Pages 6–9, 12–13, 16–19

Adding two or more numbers, such as 17,082 + 57,264 or 32,143 + 24,528 + 16,215, involves using knowledge of place value and recalling addition facts to 20.

17,082 + 57,264 = 74,346

⚠ **ALWAYS:**
Estimate
Calculate
Check

First partition both numbers into **tens of thousands**, thousands, **hundreds**, tens and ones.

Finally combine the ones, tens, **hundreds**, thousands and **tens of thousands**.

10,000s	1,000s	100s	10s	1s
10,000	1,000 1,000 1,000 1,000 1,000 / 1,000 1,000		10 10 10 10 10 / 10 10 10	1 1
10,000 10,000 10,000 10,000 10,000	1,000 1,000 1,000 1,000 1,000 / 1,000 1,000	100 100	10 10 10 10 10 / 10	1 1 1 1 1

Then add the ones.

Now add the **tens of thousands**.

Then add the thousands. As there are more than 10 thousands, we need to regroup 10 thousands into 1 **ten thousand**.

Now add the **hundreds**.

Next add the tens. As there are more than 10 tens, we need to regroup 10 tens into 1 **hundred**.

We can record this in columns.

```
    1 7 0 8 2
  + 5 7 2 6 4
            6
        1 4 0
        2 0 0
    1 4 0 0 0
    6 0 0 0 0
    7 4 3 4 6
```

leads to ➡

```
    1 7 0 8 2
  + 5 7 2 6 4
    7 4 3 4 6
      1   1
```

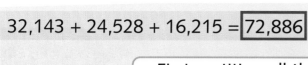

$32{,}143 + 24{,}528 + 16{,}215 = \boxed{72{,}886}$

Then add the **ones**. As there are more than 10 **ones**, we need to regroup 10 **ones** into 1 **ten**.

First partition all three numbers into **tens of thousands**, **thousands**, **hundreds**, **tens** and **ones**.

Finally combine the **ones**, **tens**, **hundreds**, **thousands** and **tens of thousands**.

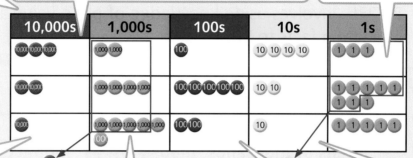

10,000s	1,000s	100s	10s	1s

Now add the **tens of thousands**.

Then add the thousands. As there are more than 10 **thousands**, we need to regroup 10 **thousands** into 1 **ten thousand**.

Now add the **hundreds**.

Next add the **tens**.

We can record this in columns.

```
  3 2 1 4 3
  2 4 5 2 8
+ 1 6 2 1 5
  ─────────
        1 6
        7 0
      8 0 0
  1 2 0 0 0
  6 0 0 0 0
  ─────────
  7 2 8 8 6
```

leads to

```
  3 2 1 4 3
  2 4 5 2 8
+ 1 6 2 1 5
  ─────────
  7 2 8 8 6
    1     1
```

Use your preferred method to work out the answers to these calculations.

34,746 + 25,108 = ☐   10,476 + 8,461 + 189 = ☐

16,387 + 8,990 = ☐   63,999 + 36,351 = ☐

Pages 76-77

Pages 6–9, 12–13, 16–19

Subtract whole numbers with more than 4 digits

Subtracting two numbers, such as 53,465 – 32,541 or 40,582 – 26,735, involves using knowledge of place value and recalling subtraction facts to 20.

53,465 – 32,541 = 20,924

⚠ **ALWAYS:**
Estimate
Calculate
Check

First **partition** 53,465 into **tens of thousands**, **thousands**, **hundreds**, **tens** and **ones**.

Then **subtract** the **ones**.

Finally place the partitioned number back together.

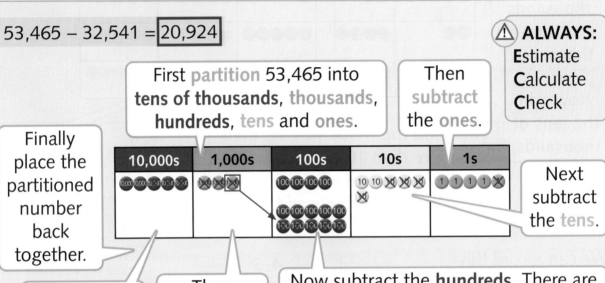

Next subtract the **tens**.

Now subtract the **tens of thousands**.

Then subtract the **thousands**.

Now subtract the **hundreds**. There are 4 **hundreds** in 53,465, and we need to subtract 5 **hundreds**. As there aren't enough **hundreds** in 53,465, **exchange** 1 **thousand** for 10 **hundreds**.

We can record this in columns.

	2,000	1,400			
50,000	3,000	400	60	5	
– 30,000	2,000	500	40	1	
20,000	0	900	20	4	

leads to

```
      2   1
  5   3   4   6   5
– 3   2   5   4   1
  2   0   9   2   4
```

20,000 + 900 + 20 + 4 = 20,924

You can also write the exchanged values like this.

```
          2  14
  5   3   4   6   5
– 3   2   5   4   1
  2   0   9   2   4
```

$40{,}582 - 26{,}735 = \boxed{13{,}847}$

First partition 40,582 into **tens of thousands**, thousands, **hundreds**, tens and ones.

Then subtract the ones. There are 2 ones in 40,582, and we need to subtract 5 ones. As there aren't enough ones in 40,582, exchange 1 ten for 10 ones.

Finally place the partitioned number back together.

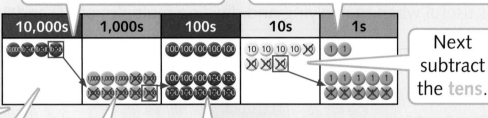

10,000s	1,000s	100s	10s	1s

Next subtract the tens.

Now subtract the **tens of thousands**.

Then subtract the thousands.

Now subtract the **hundreds**. There are 5 **hundreds** in 40,582, and we need to subtract 7 **hundreds**. As there aren't enough **hundreds** in 40,582, exchange 1 thousand for 10 **hundreds**. However, as there are no thousands in 40,582, we first need to exchange 1 **ten thousand** for 10 thousands.

We can record this in columns.

```
      30,000    9,000   1,500    70    12
      40,000      0      500     80     2                 3  9  15  7   1
    - 20,000    6,000    700     30     5     leads       4  0  5  8   2
      ------    -----    ---     --     -      to       - 2  6  7  3   5
      10,000    3,000    800     40     7                 ----------------
                                                          1  3  8  4   7
```

$10{,}000 + 3{,}000 + 800 + 40 + 7 = 13{,}847$

You can also write the exchanged values like this.

```
  3  9  15  7  12
  4  0  5   8   2
- 2  6  7   3   5
  ----------------
  1  3  8   4   7
```

Use your preferred method to work out the answers to these calculations.

$64{,}807 - 51{,}345 = \boxed{}$

$24{,}687 - 3{,}152 = \boxed{}$

$57{,}004 - 25{,}999 = \boxed{}$

$30{,}448 - 7{,}959 = \boxed{}$

Pages 78-79

Use known multiplication and division facts

Pages 6-9

Knowing about the relationship between multiplication and division, and being able to recall multiplication and division facts, is useful when multiplying and dividing multiples of 10 and 100.

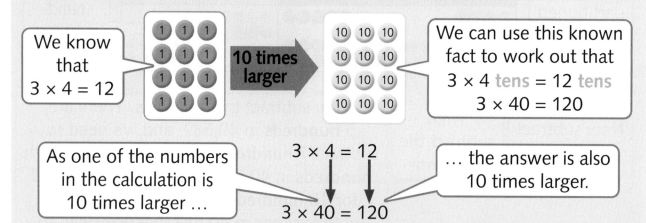

We know that
$3 \times 4 = 12$

10 times larger

We can use this known fact to work out that
3×4 tens = 12 tens
$3 \times 40 = 120$

As one of the numbers in the calculation is 10 times larger …

$3 \times 4 = 12$

$3 \times 40 = 120$

… the answer is also 10 times larger.

Multiplication is **commutative** – it can be done in any order.

Multiplication and **division** are related. If we know one multiplication or division fact, we know three other **related facts**.

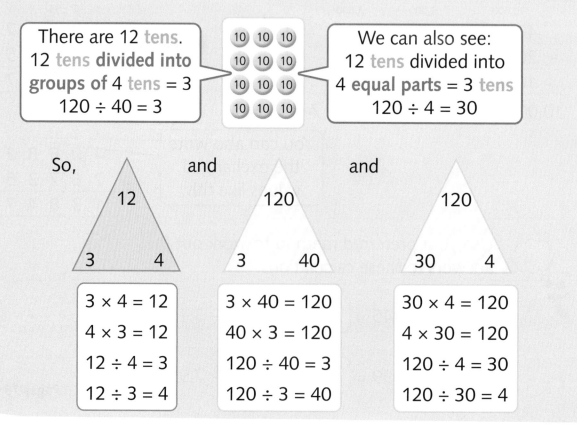

There are 12 tens.
12 tens **divided into groups of** 4 tens = 3
$120 \div 40 = 3$

We can also see:
12 tens divided into 4 **equal parts** = 3 tens
$120 \div 4 = 30$

So,

| 12 |
| 3   4 |

and

| 120 |
| 3   40 |

and

| 120 |
| 30   4 |

$3 \times 4 = 12$	$3 \times 40 = 120$	$30 \times 4 = 120$
$4 \times 3 = 12$	$40 \times 3 = 120$	$4 \times 30 = 120$
$12 \div 4 = 3$	$120 \div 40 = 3$	$120 \div 4 = 30$
$12 \div 3 = 4$	$120 \div 3 = 40$	$120 \div 30 = 4$

We can also use known multiplication tables to work out facts involving multiples of 100.

We know that 3 × 4 = 12

100 times larger

We can use this known fact to work out that
3 × 4 **hundreds** = 12 **hundreds**
3 × 400 = 1,200

As one of the numbers in the calculation is 100 times larger …

3 × 4 = 12

… the answer is also 100 times larger.

3 × 400 = 1,200

There are 12 **hundreds**.
12 **hundreds** divided into groups of 4 **hundreds** = 3
1,200 ÷ 400 = 3

We can also see:
12 **hundreds** divided into 4 equal parts = 3 **hundreds**.
1,200 ÷ 4 = 300

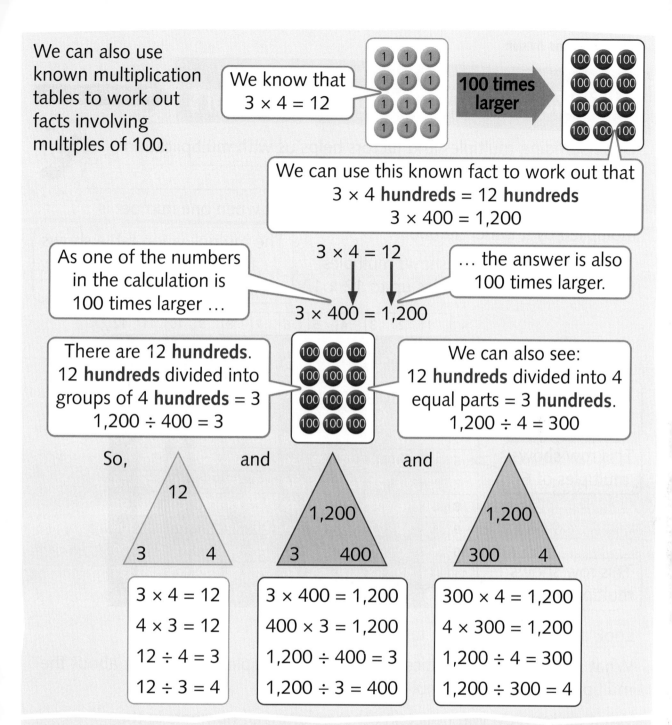

So,   and   and

| 12 | 1,200 | 1,200 |
| 3   4 | 3   400 | 300   4 |

3 × 4 = 12	3 × 400 = 1,200	300 × 4 = 1,200
4 × 3 = 12	400 × 3 = 1,200	4 × 300 = 1,200
12 ÷ 4 = 3	1,200 ÷ 400 = 3	1,200 ÷ 4 = 300
12 ÷ 3 = 4	1,200 ÷ 3 = 400	1,200 ÷ 300 = 4

We can use number lines to help when multiplying and dividing multiples of 10 and 100.

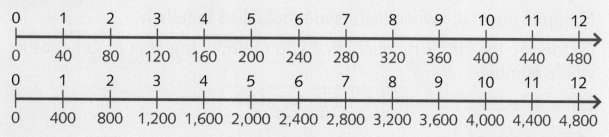

Pages 26–45, 84–87

Multiples, factors and common factors

Pages 6-7, 24-25

Understanding multiples and factors helps us with multiplication and division calculations.

A **multiple** is the result (or **product**) that we get when one number is multiplied by another number.

This multiplication table shows multiples for the **multiplication tables** up to 12 × 12.

> The multiplication table shows that 12 is a multiple of:
> 1 and 12, 2 and 6, 3 and 4.

×	1	2	3	4	5	6	7	8	9	10	11	12
1	1	2	3	4	5	6	7	8	9	10	11	(12)
2	2	4	6	8	10	(12)	14	16	18	20	22	24
3	3	6	9	(12)	15	18	21	24	27	30	33	36
4	4	8	(12)	16	20	24	28	32	36	40	44	48
5	5	10	15	20	25	30	35	40	45	50	55	60
6	6	(12)	18	24	30	36	42	48	54	60	66	72
7	7	14	21	28	35	42	49	56	63	70	77	84
8	8	16	24	32	40	48	56	64	72	80	88	96
9	9	18	27	36	45	54	63	72	81	90	99	108
10	10	20	30	40	50	60	70	80	90	100	110	120
11	11	22	33	44	55	66	77	88	99	110	121	132
12	(12)	24	36	48	60	72	84	96	108	120	132	144

This row shows multiples of 4.

This row shows multiples of 6.

This row shows multiples of 12.

Look at the multiplication table above.

What **patterns** do you notice about all the multiples of 2? What about the multiples of 5? And the multiples of 10?

What patterns do you notice in other columns of numbers in the multiplication table?

Multiples are made when **factors** are multiplied together.

Factors are the **whole numbers** that you **multiply** together to get another whole number.

factor × factor = multiple

4 is a factor of 12.

3 is a factor of 12. → 3 × 4 = 12 ← 12 is a multiple of 3 and 4.

A **factor pair** is a set of two factors. When multiplied together, they make a particular product.

Every whole number has at least one factor pair – the number 1 and itself.

Let's look at these arrays and **multiplication calculations** for the number 12.

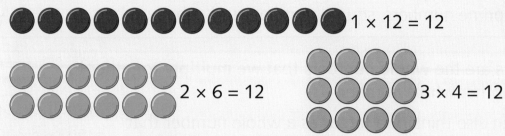

$1 \times 12 = 12$

$2 \times 6 = 12$

$3 \times 4 = 12$

We can see from the arrays that 12 has three factor pairs. It has six factors altogether.

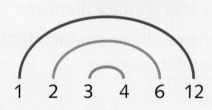

$1 \times 12 = 12$

$2 \times 6 = 12$

$3 \times 4 = 12$

So, the factors of 12 are 1, 2, 3, 4, 6 and 12.

We can also think of a factor as a whole number that **divides exactly into** another number.

multiple ÷ factor = factor

4 is a factor of 12.

12 is a multiple of 3 and 4. $12 \div 4 = 3$ 3 is a factor of 12.

Common factors are factors that are shared by two or more numbers.

We know that the factors of 12 are 1, 2, 3, 4, 6 and 12.

The factors of 20 are: So, 1, 2 and 4 are common factors of 12 and 20.

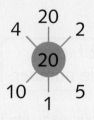

We can see from this **Venn diagram** that the **highest common factor** (HCF) of 12 and 20 is 4.

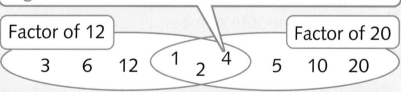

Factor of 12   Factor of 20

3   6   12   1   2   4   5   10   20

Write

Find the common factors for each pair of numbers.

| 10 | and | 15 | | 20 | and | 24 | | 12 | and | 15 |

Pages 28-45, 52-59

Primes, squares and cubes

Pages 6-7, 24-27

In our number system there are some special types of numbers called prime numbers, square numbers and cube numbers.

Factors are the **whole numbers** that we **multiply** together to get another whole number.

We can also think of a factor as a whole number that **divides exactly into** another number.

A **multiple** is the result (or **product**) that we get when one number is multiplied by another number.

Prime numbers

Numbers that have only two factors – 1 and itself – are called prime numbers.

Numbers with more than two factors are called **composite numbers**.

The number 1 is not a prime number as it does not have exactly two factors – it only has one factor: 1.

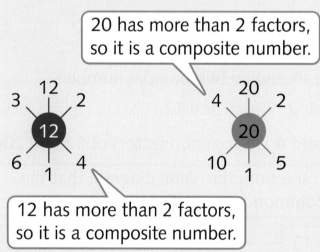

20 has more than 2 factors, so it is a composite number.

12 has more than 2 factors, so it is a composite number.

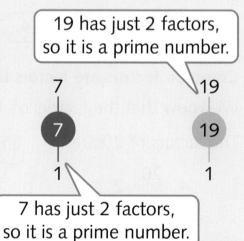

19 has just 2 factors, so it is a prime number.

7 has just 2 factors, so it is a prime number.

To prove that a number less than 100 is a prime number, it is enough to show the number is not **divisible** by a 1-digit number other than 1.

Write

Use your knowledge of multiples and factors to decide whether each of these numbers is a prime number.

9	11	13
15	17	21

Square numbers

When we multiply a whole number by itself, the result (or product) is a square number, for example: $3 \times 3 = 9$.

Square numbers have a special symbol, a small '2' after the number, like this: 3^2.

Square numbers can be represented by a square **array**.

These are the first six square numbers.

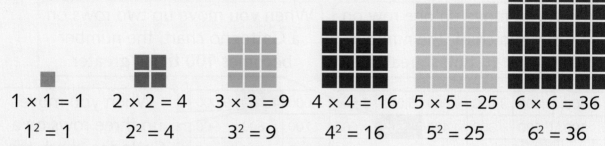

$1 \times 1 = 1$	$2 \times 2 = 4$	$3 \times 3 = 9$	$4 \times 4 = 16$	$5 \times 5 = 25$	$6 \times 6 = 36$
$1^2 = 1$	$2^2 = 4$	$3^2 = 9$	$4^2 = 16$	$5^2 = 25$	$6^2 = 36$

Look at the multiplication table on page 26.

What are all the square numbers up to 12×12?

Cube numbers

A cube number is the result of multiplying a whole number by itself three times, for example $3 \times 3 \times 3 = 27$.

Cube numbers have a special symbol, a small '3' after the number, like this: 3^3.

If you multiply a number by itself, then itself again, the result is a cube number. So you can use a square number to find a cube number.

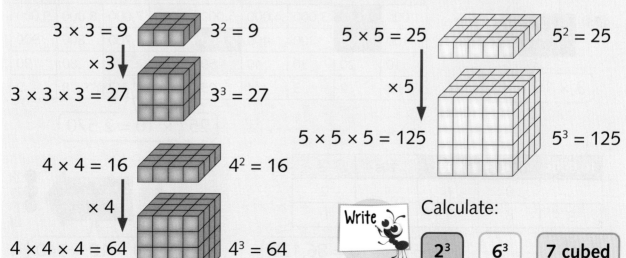

$3 \times 3 = 9$ $3^2 = 9$

$\times 3$

$3 \times 3 \times 3 = 27$ $3^3 = 27$

$5 \times 5 = 25$ $5^2 = 25$

$\times 5$

$5 \times 5 \times 5 = 125$ $5^3 = 125$

$4 \times 4 = 16$ $4^2 = 16$

$\times 4$

$4 \times 4 \times 4 = 64$ $4^3 = 64$

Write

Calculate:

2^3 6^3 **7 cubed**

Multiply whole numbers by 10, 100 and 1,000

Pages 6-9, 24-27

Knowing how to multiply a whole number by 10, 100 and 1,000 is useful when multiplying larger numbers. It's important to understand what happens to the place value of the digits when you multiply by 10, 100 or 1,000.

When you move up one row on a Gattegno chart, the number becomes **10 times greater**.

When you move up two rows on a Gattegno chart, the number becomes **100 times greater**.

When you move up three rows on a Gattegno chart, the number becomes **1,000 times greater**.

1,000	2,000	3,000	4,000	5,000	6,000	7,000	8,000	9,000
100	200	300	400	500	600	700	800	900
10	20	30	40	50	60	70	80	90
1	2	3	4	5	6	7	8	9

$2 \times 10 = 20$ $5 \times 100 = 500$ $8 \times 1,000 = 8,000$

Multiplying by 10

When we **multiply** a **whole number** by 10, the **value** of each **digit** in the number becomes 10 times greater and the digits move one **place value** to the left. We include a **zero** in the **ones** place to act as a **place holder**.

100s	10s	1s
		7
	7	0

$7 \times 10 = 70$

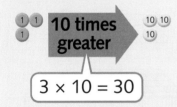

10 times greater

$3 \times 10 = 30$

1,000	2,000	3,000	4,000	5,000	6,000	7,000	8,000	9,000
100	200	300	400	500	600	700	800	900
10	20	30	40	50	60	70	80	90
1	2	3	4	5	6	7	8	9

$257 \times 10 = 2,570$

10,000s	1,000s	100s	10s	1s
	8	6	1	2
8	6	1	2	0

$8,612 \times 10 = 86,120$

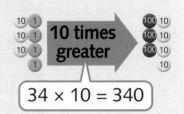

10 times greater

$34 \times 10 = 340$

Multiplying by 100

When we multiply a whole number by 100, the value of each digit in the number becomes 100 times greater and the digits move two place values to the left. We include zeros in the tens and ones places to act as place holders.

1,000s	100s	10s	1s
			9
	9	0	0

$9 \times 100 = 900$

$36 \times 100 = 3,600$

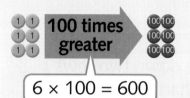

$6 \times 100 = 600$

1,000	2,000	3,000	4,000	5,000	6,000	7,000	8,000	9,000
100	200	300	400	500	600	700	800	900
10	20	30	40	50	60	70	80	90
1	2	3	4	5	6	7	8	9

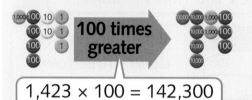

100 times greater

$1,423 \times 100 = 142,300$

10,000s	1,000s	100s	10s	1s
		4	8	3
4	8	3	0	0

$483 \times 100 = 48,300$

Multiplying by 1,000

When we multiply a whole number by 1,000, the value of each digit in the number becomes 1,000 times greater and the digits move three place values to the left. We include zeros in the **hundreds**, tens and ones places to act as place holders.

1,000s	100s	10s	1s
			8
8	0	0	0

$8 \times 1,000 = 8,000$

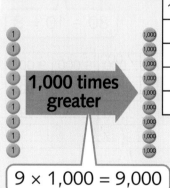

1,000 times greater

10,000	20,000	30,000	40,000	50,000	60,000	70,000	80,000	90,000
1,000	2,000	3,000	4,000	5,000	6,000	7,000	8,000	9,000
100	200	300	400	500	600	700	800	900
10	20	30	40	50	60	70	80	90
1	2	3	4	5	6	7	8	9

$28 \times 1,000 = 28,000$

$9 \times 1,000 = 9,000$

 1,000 times greater

$231 \times 1,000 = 231,000$

$549 \times 1,000 = 549,000$

100,000s	10,000s	1,000s	100s	10s	1s
			5	4	9
5	4	9	0	0	0

Pages 32–41, 80–81

Divide whole numbers by 10, 100 and 1,000

Pages 6-9, 24-27, 30-31

Knowing how to divide a whole number by 10, 100 and 1,000 is useful when dividing larger numbers. It's important to understand what happens to the place value of the digits when you divide by 10, 100 or 1,000.

When you move down one row on a Gattegno chart, the number becomes **10 times smaller**.

When you move down two rows on a Gattegno chart, the number becomes **100 times smaller**.

When you move down three rows on a Gattegno chart, the number becomes **1,000 times smaller**.

1,000	2,000	3,000	4,000	5,000	6,000	7,000	8,000	9,000
100	200	300	400	500	600	700	800	900
10	20	30	40	50	60	70	80	90
1	2	3	4	5	6	7	8	9

$20 \div 10 = 2$

$500 \div 100 = 5$

$9,000 \div 1,000 = 9$

Dividing by 10

When we **divide** a **multiple of 10** by 10, the **value** of each **digit** in the number becomes 10 times smaller and the digits move one **place value** to the right. We remove the **zero** from the **ones** place.

100s	10s	1s
	8	0
		8

$80 \div 10 = 8$

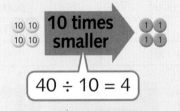

10 times smaller

$40 \div 10 = 4$

1,000	2,000	3,000	4,000	5,000	6,000	7,000	8,000	9,000
100	200	300	400	500	600	700	800	900
10	20	30	40	50	60	70	80	90
1	2	3	4	5	6	7	8	9

$3,680 \div 10 = 368$

10,000s	1,000s	100s	10s	1s
1	2	6	8	0
	1	2	6	8

$12,680 \div 10 = 1,268$

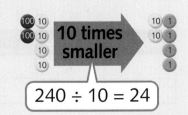

10 times smaller

$240 \div 10 = 24$

Dividing by 100

When we divide a **multiple of 100** by 100, the value of each digit in the number becomes 100 times smaller and the digits move two place values to the right. We remove the zeros from the tens and ones places.

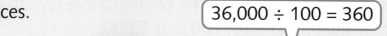

1,000s	100s	10s	1s
	2	0	0
			2

$200 \div 100 = 2$

$36,000 \div 100 = 360$

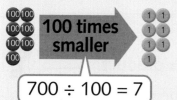

100 times smaller

$700 \div 100 = 7$

10,000	20,000	30,000	40,000	50,000	60,000	70,000	80,000	90,000
1,000	2,000	3,000	4,000	5,000	6,000	7,000	8,000	9,000
100	200	300	400	500	600	700	800	900
10	20	30	40	50	60	70	80	90
1	2	3	4	5	6	7	8	9

100 times smaller

$3,200 \div 100 = 32$

100,000s	10,000s	1,000s	100s	10s	1s
6	4	3	7	0	0
		6	4	3	7

$643,700 \div 100 = 6,437$

Dividing by 1,000

When we divide a **multiple of 1,000** by 1,000, the value of each digit in the number becomes 1,000 times smaller and the digits move three place values to the right. We remove the zeros from the **hundreds**, tens and ones places.

1,000s	100s	10s	1s
3	0	0	0
			3

$3,000 \div 1,000 = 3$

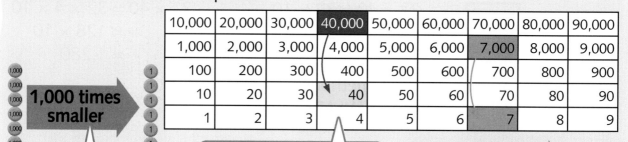

10,000	20,000	30,000	40,000	50,000	60,000	70,000	80,000	90,000
1,000	2,000	3,000	4,000	5,000	6,000	7,000	8,000	9,000
100	200	300	400	500	600	700	800	900
10	20	30	40	50	60	70	80	90
1	2	3	4	5	6	7	8	9

1,000 times smaller

$6,000 \div 1,000 = 6$

$47,000 \div 1,000 = 47$

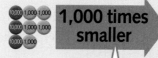

1,000 times smaller

$35,000 \div 1,000 = 35$

$856,000 \div 1,000 = 856$

100,000s	10,000s	1,000s	100s	10s	1s
8	5	6	0	0	0
			8	5	6

Pages 34-35, 42-45, 82-83

Pages 6–9, 24–27, 30-33

Multiply and divide by multiples of 10, 100 and 1,000

We can apply our knowledge of the multiplication tables, and what we know about factors and the commutative law, to multiply and divide by multiples of 10, 100 and 1,000.

A **factor** is a **whole number** that **divides exactly into** another number.

factor × factor = **product**

Remember

Multiplication and **division** are related. If we know one multiplication or division fact, we know three other related facts.

Multiplication has three properties:

Commutative property
Changing the order of the factors does not change the product.

Associative property
Changing the grouping of the factors does not change the product.

Distributive property
A multiplication calculation can be **partitioned** into the sum of two or more smaller calculations.

We can use these properties to help multiply by multiples of 10, 100 and 1,000.

32 × 40 = 1,280

$$32 \times 40 = 32 \times 10 \times 4$$
$$= 320 \times 4$$
$$= 1,280$$

$$32 \times 40 = 32 \times 4 \times 10$$
$$= 128 \times 10$$
$$= 1,280$$

What's the same about these methods? What's different?
Which method do you prefer? Why?

We can also use known facts to help work out related facts.

28 × 5 = 140

How else could you work out the answer to each of these calculations?

$$28 \times 50 = 28 \times 5 \times 10$$
$$= 140 \times 10$$
$$= 1,400$$

$$280 \times 5 = 28 \times 5 \times 10$$
$$= 140 \times 10$$
$$= 1,400$$

$$28 \times 500 = 28 \times 5 \times 100$$
$$= 140 \times 100$$
$$= 14,000$$

$$280 \times 500 = 28 \times 5 \times 1,000$$
$$= 140 \times 1,000$$
$$= 140,000$$

We can use the relationship between multiplication and division, mental strategies and known division facts to help us divide by multiples of 10, 100 and 1,000.

$4,800 \div 60 = \boxed{80}$

$4,800 \div 60$
↓
$4,800 \div 10 = 480$
↓
$480 \div 6 = 80$

$4,800 \div 60$
↓
$4,800 \div 6 = 800$
↓
$800 \div 10 = 80$

What's the same about these methods? What's different?
Which method do you prefer? Why?

We can use a similar strategy to work out these divisions.

$3,600 \div 400 = \boxed{9}$

$3,600 \div 400$
↓
$3,600 \div 100 = 36$
↓
$36 \div 4 = 9$

$63,000 \div 90 = \boxed{700}$

$63,000 \div 90$
↓
$63,000 \div 10 = 6,300$
↓
$6,300 \div 9 = 700$

$18,000 \div 300 = \boxed{60}$

$18,000 \div 300$
↓
$18,000 \div 100 = 180$
↓
$180 \div 3 = 60$

How else could you work out the answer to each of the above calculations?

  Use the properties of multiplication and known facts to work out the answers to these calculations. Show all the steps in your thinking.

$700 \times 400 = \boxed{}$ $60 \times 7,000 = \boxed{}$ $80 \times 400 = \boxed{}$

$240 \times 300 = \boxed{}$ $54 \times 6,000 = \boxed{}$ $1,200 \times 500 = \boxed{}$

$1,900 \div 5 = \boxed{}$ $4,200 \div 30 = \boxed{}$ $24,000 \div 400 = \boxed{}$

$48,000 \div 60 = \boxed{}$ $58,000 \div 200 = \boxed{}$ $9,600 \div 120 = \boxed{}$

 Compare your answers to the calculations above with a partner, and talk about the strategies you used.

Which strategies were the most effective and efficient?

Pages 36-45

35

Multiply up to a 4-digit number by a 1-digit number

Pages 6-9, 12-13, 24-27 30-31, 34-35

We can use our understanding of place value and multiplication tables facts to multiply a 2-, 3- or 4-digit number by a 1-digit number, such as 3,264 × 3.

3,264 × 3 = $\boxed{9,792}$

⚠ **ALWAYS:**
Estimate
Calculate
Check

Step 1: Set out the calculation.

×	3,000	200	60	4
3	1,000 1,000 1,000	100 100	10 10 10 10 10 10	1 1 1 1
	1,000 1,000 1,000	100 100	10 10 10 10 10 10	1 1 1 1
	1,000 1,000 1,000	100 100	10 10 10 10 10 10	1 1 1 1

As we are multiplying 3,264 by 3, **partition** 3 lots of 3,264 into thousands, **hundreds**, tens and ones.

Step 2: Multiply the ones.

×	3,000	200	60	4
3	1,000 1,000 1,000	100 100	10 10 10 10 10 10	1 1 1 1
	1,000 1,000 1,000	100 100	10 10 10 10 10 10	1 1 1 1
	1,000 1,000 1,000	100 100	10 10 10 10 10 10	1 1 1 1

10

4 ones **multiplied by** 3 (4 × 3). As there are more than 10 ones, we need to **regroup** 10 ones into 1 ten.

Step 3: Multiply the tens.

×	3,000	200	60	4
3	1,000 1,000 1,000	100 100	10 10 10 10 10 10	
	1,000 1,000 1,000	100 100	10 10 10 10 10 10	
	1,000 1,000 1,000	100 100	10 10 10 10 10 10	1 1

100   10

6 tens multiplied by 3 (60 × 3). As there are more than 10 tens, we need to regroup 10 tens into 1 **hundred**.

Step 4: Multiply the hundreds.

×	3,000	200	60	4
3	1,000 1,000 1,000	100 100		
	1,000 1,000 1,000	100 100	10 10	
	1,000 1,000 1,000	100 100	10 10 10 10 10 10	1 1

100   10

2 **hundreds** multiplied by 3 (200 × 3).

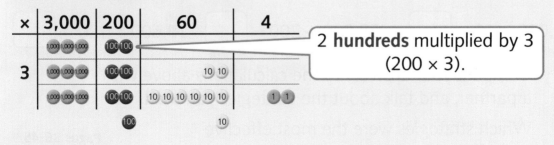

Step 5: Multiply the thousands.

×	3,000	200	60	4

> 3 thousands multiplied by 3 (3,000 × 3).

Step 6: Combine the thousands, hundreds, tens and ones.

×	3,000	200	60	4

9 thousands + 7 hundreds + 9 tens + 2 ones = 9,792
9,000 + 700 + 90 + 2 = 9,792

We can record this calculation in different ways.

Grid method

×	3,000	200	60	4	
3	9,000	600	180	12	= 9,792

Partitioning method

$3,264 × 3 = (3,000 × 3) + (200 × 3) + (60 × 3) + (4 × 3)$

$\qquad\qquad = 9,000 + 600 + 180 + 12$

$\qquad\qquad = 9,792$

What's the same about each of these methods?

What's different?

Which method do you prefer? Why?

Expanded written method

```
   3 2 6 4
×        3
_____
     1 2   (4 × 3)
   1 8 0   (60 × 3)
   6 0 0   (200 × 3)
 9 0 0 0   (3,000 × 3)
_____
 9 7 9 2
```

leads to

Formal written method of short multiplication

```
   3 2 6 4
×        3
_____
   9 7 9 2
     1   1
```

```
   3 2 6 4
×    ₁ ₁ 3
_____
   9 7 9 2
```

You can also write the regrouped values like this.

Pages 38–41

Multiply a 2-digit number by a 2-digit number

Pages 6-9, 12-13, 24-27 30-31, 34-37

To multiply a pair of 2-digit numbers, such as 27 × 34, we can partition both numbers, multiply the tens and ones digits in one number by the tens and ones digits in the other number and then add the partial products.

27 × 34 = **918**

⚠ **ALWAYS:**
Estimate
Calculate
Check

Step 1: Set out the calculation.

and Step 2: Multiply the ones digit by the ones digit.

×	20	7
30		
4		🔴🔴🔴🔴🔴🔴🔴

Grid method

×	20	7
30		
4		**28**

Expanded written method   leads to ➡   **Formal written method of long multiplication**

```
    2 7
×   3 4
    2 8   (7 × 4)
```

```
      2 7
×     3 4
    ²8     (27 × 4)
```

Regroup the 2 tens.

Step 3: Multiply the tens digit by the ones digit.

×	20	7
30		
4	10 10 / 10 10 / 10 10 / 10 10	🔴🔴🔴🔴🔴🔴🔴

×	20	7
30		
4	**80**	28

```
    2 7
×   3 4
    2 8   (7 × 4)
    8 0   (20 × 4)
```

leads to ➡

```
      2 7
×     3 4
  1 0²8     (27 × 4)
```

Add the regrouped tens.

Step 4: Multiply the ones digit by the tens digit.

×	20	7
30		10 10 10 10 10 10 10 10 10 10 10 10 10 10 10 10 10 10 10 10 10
4	10 10 10 10 10 10 10 10	1 1 1 1 1 1 1 1 1 1 1 1 1 1 1 1 1 1 1 1 1 1 1 1 1 1 1 1

```
      2 7
  ×   3 4
      2 8   (7 × 4)
      8 0   (20 × 4)
    2 1 0   (7 × 30)
```

leads to ➡

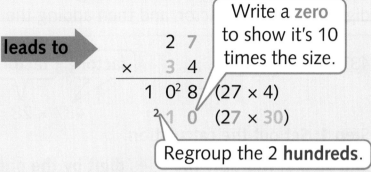

×	20	7
30		210
4	80	28

> Write a **zero** to show it's 10 times the size.

```
      2 7
  ×   3 4
    1 0² 8   (27 × 4)
    ² 1 0   (27 × 30)
```

> Regroup the 2 **hundreds**.

Step 5: Multiply the tens digit by the tens digit.

×	20	7
30	100 100 100 100 100 100	10 10 10 10 10 10 10 10 10 10 10 10 10 10 10 10 10 10 10 10 10
4	10 10 10 10 10 10 10 10	1 1 1 1 1 1 1 1 1 1 1 1 1 1 1 1 1 1 1 1 1 1 1 1 1 1 1 1

```
      2 7
  ×   3 4
      2 8   (7 × 4)
      8 0   (20 × 4)
    2 1 0   (7 × 30)
    6 0 0   (20 × 30)
```

leads to ➡

×	20	7
30	600	210
4	80	28

```
      2 7
  ×   3 4
    1 0² 8   (27 × 4)
    8² 1 0   (27 × 30)
```

> Add the regrouped **hundreds**.

Step 6: Add the partial products.

×	20	7
30	600	210
4	80	28

600 + 210 + 80 + 28 = 918

```
      2 7
  ×   3 4
      2 8   (7 × 4)
      8 0   (20 × 4)
    2 1 0   (7 × 30)
    6 0 0   (20 × 30)
    9 1 8
      1
```

leads to ➡

```
      2 7
  ×   3 4
    1 0² 8   (27 × 4)
    8² 1 0   (27 × 30)
      9 1 8
```

Pages 40–41

Pages 6-9, 12-13, 24-27 30-31, 34-39

Multiply a 3- or 4-digit number by a 2-digit number

Multiplying a 3- or 4-digit number by a 2-digit number is similar to multiplying a pair of 2-digit numbers. It involves partitioning both numbers, multiplying each of the digits in one factor by each of the digits in the other factor, and then adding the partial products.

$437 \times 28 = \boxed{12{,}236}$

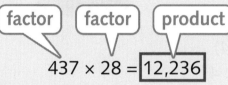

$437 \times 28 = \boxed{12{,}236}$

⚠ **ALWAYS:**
Estimate
Calculate
Check

Step 1: Set out the calculation.

and Step 2: Multiply the ones digit by the ones digit.

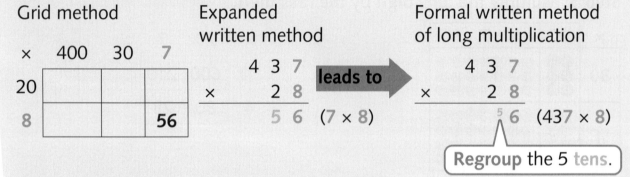

Grid method

×	400	30	7
20			
8			56

Expanded written method

```
    4 3 7
  ×   2 8
        leads to
    5 6  (7 × 8)
```

Formal written method of long multiplication

```
    4 3 7
  ×   2 8
    ⁵6  (437 × 8)
```

Regroup the 5 **tens**.

Step 3: Multiply the tens digit by the ones digit.

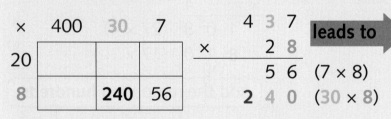

×	400	30	7
20			
8		240	56

```
    4 3 7
  ×   2 8
        leads to
    5 6  (7 × 8)
  2 4 0  (30 × 8)
```

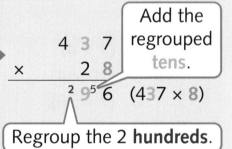

Add the regrouped **tens**.

```
    4 3 7
  ×   2 8
  ² 9⁵ 6  (437 × 8)
```

Regroup the 2 **hundreds**.

Step 4: Multiply the hundreds digit by the ones digit.

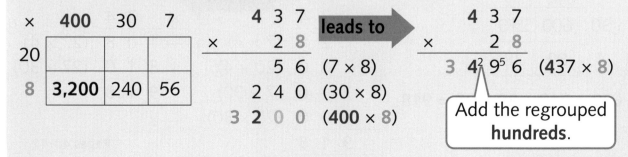

×	400	30	7
20			
8	3,200	240	56

```
    4 3 7
  ×   2 8
        leads to
    5 6  (7 × 8)
  2 4 0  (30 × 8)
3 2 0 0  (400 × 8)
```

```
    4 3 7
  ×   2 8
3 4² 9⁵ 6  (437 × 8)
```

Add the regrouped **hundreds**.

Step 5: Multiply the ones digit by the tens digit.

×	400	30	7
20			**140**
8	3,200	240	56

```
    4 3 7
×     2 8
    _____
    5 6   (7 × 8)
  2 4 0   (30 × 8)
3 2 0 0   (400 × 8)
  1 4 0   (7 × 20)
```

leads to

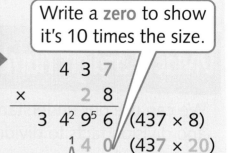

Write a **zero** to show it's 10 times the size.

```
      4 3 7
×       2 8
    _____
3 4² 9⁵ 6   (437 × 8)
    1 4 0    (437 × 20)
```

Regroup the 1 **hundred**.

Step 6: Multiply the tens digit by the tens digit.

×	400	30	7
20		**600**	140
8	3,200	240	56

```
    4 3 7
×     2 8
    _____
    5 6   (7 × 8)
  2 4 0   (30 × 8)
3 2 0 0   (400 × 8)
  1 4 0   (7 × 20)
  6 0 0   (30 × 20)
```

leads to

```
      4 3 7
×       2 8
    _____
3 4² 9⁵ 6   (437 × 8)
7¹ 4 0   (437 × 20)
```

Add the regrouped **hundred**.

Step 7: Multiply the hundreds digit by the tens digit.

×	400	30	7
20	**8,000**	600	140
8	3,200	240	56

```
    4 3 7
×     2 8
    _____
    5 6   (7 × 8)
  2 4 0   (30 × 8)
3 2 0 0   (400 × 8)
  1 4 0   (7 × 20)
  6 0 0   (30 × 20)
8 0 0 0   (400 × 20)
```

leads to

```
      4 3 7
×       2 8
    _____
3 4² 9⁵ 6   (437 × 8)
8 7¹ 4 0   (437 × 20)
```

Step 8: Add the partial products.

×	400	30	7
20	8,000	600	140
8	3,200	240	56

8,740 + 3,496 = 12,236

```
    4 3 7
×     2 8
    _____
    5 6   (7 × 8)
  2 4 0   (30 × 8)
3 2 0 0   (400 × 8)
  1 4 0   (7 × 20)
  6 0 0   (30 × 20)
8 0 0 0   (400 × 20)
_____
1 2 2 3 6
  1   1
```

leads to

```
      4 3 7
×       2 8
    _____
3 4² 9⁵ 6   (437 × 8)
8 7¹ 4 0   (437 × 20)
_____
1 2 2 3 6
  1   1
```

41

Divide a 3-digit number by a 1-digit number

Pages 6–9, 12–13, 24–27, 32–35

We can use our understanding of place value and multiplication and division facts to divide a 3-digit number by a 1-digit number, such as 321 ÷ 6.

321 ÷ 6 = 53 r 3   We can **decompose** or **regroup** 321.

⚠ **ALWAYS:**
Estimate
Calculate
Check

The **quotient** is the answer to a division calculation.

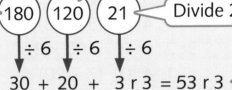

Divide 180 by 6. Divide 120 by 6. Divide 21 by 6.

÷ 6   ÷ 6   ÷ 6

30 + 20 + 3 r 3 = 53 r 3

Add the three quotients to give you the answer.

🐜 Remember   We can regroup numbers in different ways.

We can also regroup 321 like this.

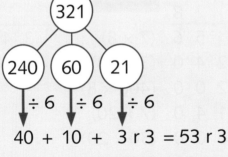

40 + 10 + 3 r 3 = 53 r 3

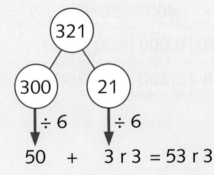

50 + 3 r 3 = 53 r 3

How else could you regroup 321 to work out the answer to this division calculation?

We can represent this with place value counters.

Step 1: Set out the calculation.

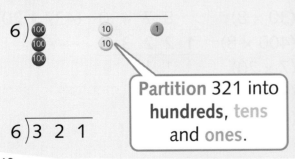

Partition 321 into **hundreds**, tens and ones.

$6\overline{)3\ 2\ 1}$

Step 2: Share the hundreds.

Divide the **hundreds** into groups of 6.

0
$6\overline{)3\ 2\ 1}$

There are 0 groups of **6 hundreds** in 300.

Step 3: Exchange the hundreds.

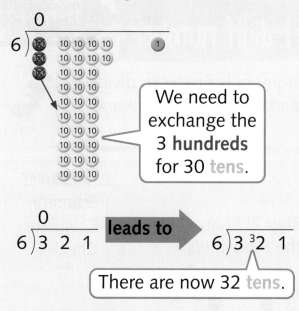

We need to exchange the 3 **hundreds** for 30 tens.

$$6\overline{)3\ \ 2\ \ 1}$$ **leads to** $$6\overline{)3\ {}^32\ \ 1}$$

There are now 32 tens.

Step 4: Share the tens.

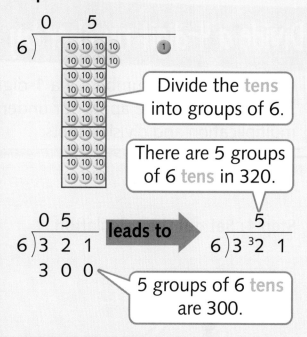

Divide the tens into groups of 6.

There are 5 groups of 6 tens in 320.

$$6\overline{)3\ \ 2\ \ 1}$$
$$3\ \ 0\ \ 0$$
leads to
$$6\overline{)3\ {}^32\ \ 1}$$

5 groups of 6 tens are 300.

Step 5: Exchange the tens.

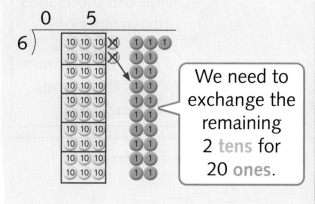

We need to exchange the remaining 2 tens for 20 ones.

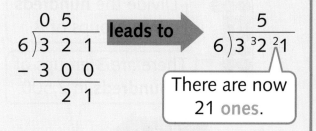

$$6\overline{)3\ \ 2\ \ 1}$$
$$-\ 3\ \ 0\ \ 0$$
$$\ \ \ \ \ \ 2\ \ 1$$
leads to
$$6\overline{)3\ {}^32\ {}^21}$$

There are now 21 ones.

Step 6: Share the ones.

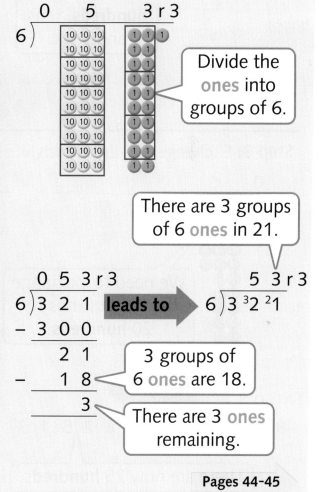

Divide the ones into groups of 6.

There are 3 groups of 6 ones in 21.

$$6\overline{)3\ \ 2\ \ 1}$$
$$-\ 3\ \ 0\ \ 0$$
$$\ \ \ \ \ \ 2\ \ 1$$
$$-\ \ \ \ \ 1\ \ 8$$
$$\ \ \ \ \ \ \ \ \ \ 3$$
leads to
$$6\overline{)3\ {}^32\ {}^21}$$ 5 3 r 3

3 groups of 6 ones are 18.

There are 3 ones remaining.

Pages 44-45

Divide a 4-digit number by a 1-digit number

Pages 6-9, 12-13, 24-27 32-35, 42-43

Dividing a 4-digit number by a 1-digit number is similar to dividing 3-digit numbers: we apply our understanding of place value and multiplication and division facts.

$2,513 \div 8 = \boxed{314 \text{ r } 1}$

⚠ ALWAYS:
Estimate
Calculate
Check

Step 1: Set out the calculation.

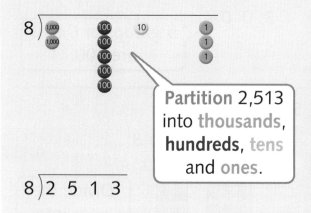

Partition 2,513 into thousands, hundreds, tens and ones.

$8\overline{)2\ 5\ 1\ 3}$

Step 2: Share the thousands.

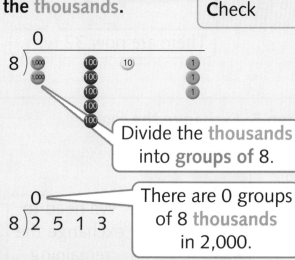

Divide the thousands into groups of 8.

There are 0 groups of 8 thousands in 2,000.

$\overset{0}{8\overline{)2\ 5\ 1\ 3}}$

Step 3: Exchange the thousands.

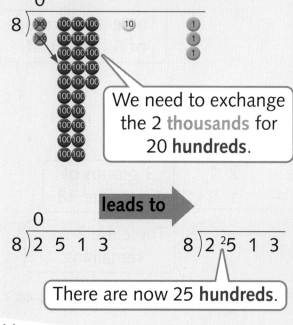

We need to exchange the 2 thousands for 20 hundreds.

$\overset{0}{8\overline{)2\ 5\ 1\ 3}}$ **leads to** $8\overline{)2\,^25\ 1\ 3}$

There are now 25 hundreds.

Step 4: Share the hundreds.

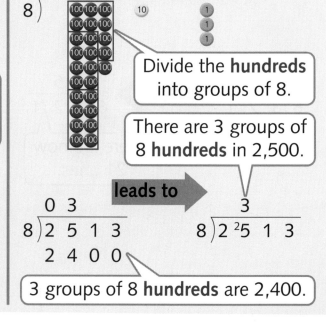

Divide the hundreds into groups of 8.

There are 3 groups of 8 hundreds in 2,500.

$\overset{0\ \ 3}{8\overline{)2\ 5\ 1\ 3}}$
$\ \ \ \ 2\ 4\ 0\ 0$

leads to

$\overset{\ \ 3}{8\overline{)2\,^25\ 1\ 3}}$

3 groups of 8 hundreds are 2,400.

Step 5: Exchange the hundreds.

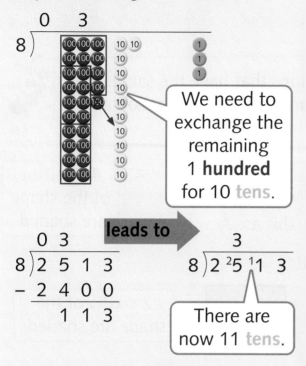

We need to exchange the remaining 1 **hundred** for 10 tens.

leads to

```
    0 3              3
8)2 5 1 3        8)2 ²5 ¹1 3
- 2 4 0 0
    1 1 3
```

There are now 11 tens.

Step 6: Share the tens.

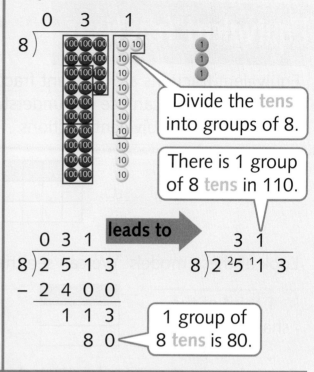

Divide the tens into groups of 8.

There is 1 group of 8 tens in 110.

leads to

```
    0 3 1            3 1
8)2 5 1 3        8)2 ²5 ¹1 3
- 2 4 0 0
    1 1 3
      8 0
```

1 group of 8 tens is 80.

Step 7: Exchange the tens.

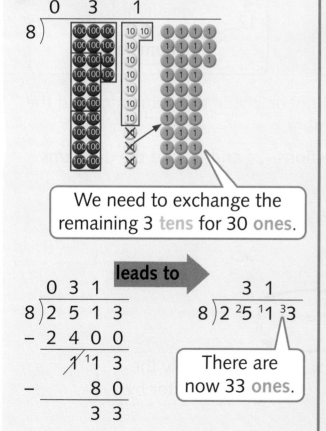

We need to exchange the remaining 3 tens for 30 ones.

leads to

```
    0 3 1            3 1
8)2 5 1 3        8)2 ²5 ¹1 ³3
- 2 4 0 0
    ↗1 ¹1 3
-      8 0
       3 3
```

There are now 33 ones.

Step 8: Share the ones.

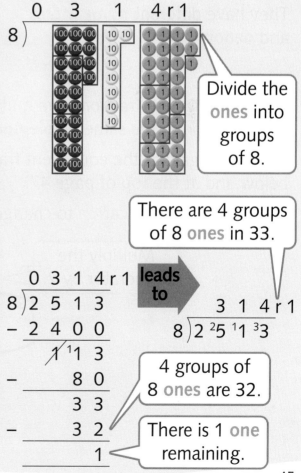

Divide the ones into groups of 8.

There are 4 groups of 8 ones in 33.

leads to

```
    0 3 1 4 r 1
8)2 5 1 3              3 1 4 r 1
- 2 4 0 0         8)2 ²5 ¹1 ³3
   ↗1 ¹1 3
-      8 0
       3 3
-      3 2
         1
```

4 groups of 8 ones are 32.

There is 1 one remaining.

Equivalent fractions

Equivalent fractions are different fractions that have the same, or equal, value. We can use our understanding of multiplication and division to find equivalent fractions.

Look at this model.
There are 12 equal parts.

We can say that:

We can write this as: $\frac{4}{12}$

4 twelfths of the shape are shaded.

Look at these models. We can see that: $\frac{1}{3} = \frac{2}{6} = \frac{4}{12}$

1 third of the shape is shaded.

2 sixths of the shape are shaded.

Equivalent fractions are fractions that have the same, or equal, value.

They have different numerators and denominators.

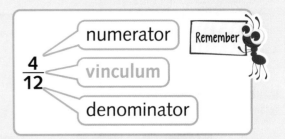

numerator

vinculum

Remember

$\frac{4}{12}$

denominator

To find equivalent fractions, we multiply or divide the numerator and the denominator by the same whole number.

Let's look again at the equivalent fractions $\frac{1}{3}$, $\frac{2}{6}$ and $\frac{4}{12}$, and the diagrams below and at the top of page 47.

We can use multiplication to change $\frac{1}{3}$ so that it is equivalent to $\frac{2}{6}$.

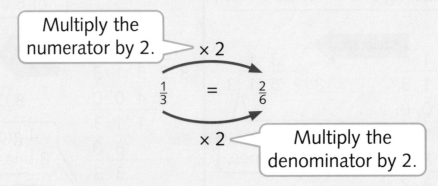

Multiply the numerator by 2.

× 2

$\frac{1}{3}$ = $\frac{2}{6}$

× 2

Multiply the denominator by 2.

We can use **division** to change $\frac{4}{12}$ so that it is equivalent to $\frac{2}{6}$.

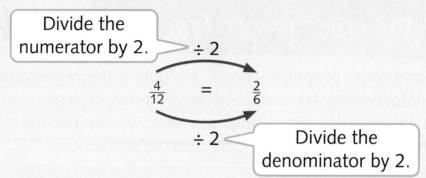

Divide the numerator by 2.
÷ 2

$$\frac{4}{12} = \frac{2}{6}$$

÷ 2
Divide the denominator by 2.

Draw Draw a diagram similar to that above to show that $\frac{4}{12} = \frac{1}{3}$.

In the same way, we can use these models to find equivalent fractions.

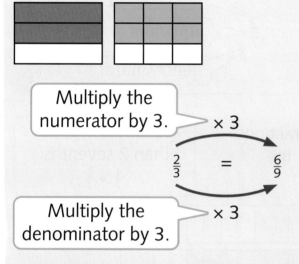

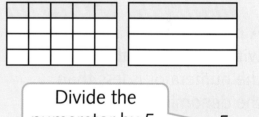

Multiply the numerator by 3.
× 3

$$\frac{2}{3} = \frac{6}{9}$$

× 3
Multiply the denominator by 3.

What other fractions are equivalent to $\frac{2}{3}$?

Divide the numerator by 5.
÷ 5

$$\frac{5}{20} = \frac{1}{4}$$

÷ 5
Divide the denominator by 5.

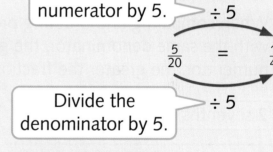

What other fractions are equivalent to $\frac{1}{4}$?

Draw Draw models or diagrams to show equivalent fractions for each of these **unit fractions**.

 $\frac{1}{2}$ $\frac{1}{8}$ $\frac{1}{5}$ $\frac{1}{10}$

Draw Draw models or diagrams to show equivalent fractions for each of these **non-unit fractions**.

 $\frac{3}{4}$ $\frac{8}{10}$ $\frac{5}{6}$ $\frac{3}{5}$

Pages 48-63

Compare and order proper fractions

Pages 46-47

To compare and order proper fractions, we look at the numerators and denominators of the fractions and apply knowledge of equivalent fractions. Like with whole numbers, we can use the inequality symbols < and > to compare and order fractions.

We can order fractions:

in **ascending** order – from **smallest** to **largest/greatest**

or in **descending** order – from **largest/greatest** to smallest.

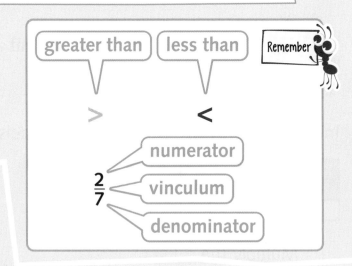

greater than | less than | Remember

> <

numerator

$\frac{2}{7}$ vinculum

denominator

A **proper fraction** is a fraction with a value less than 1, where the numerator is less than the denominator.

When comparing and ordering proper fractions with the same denominator, the **greater** the numerator, the greater the fraction.

4 sevenths is greater than 2 sevenths.
$\frac{4}{7} > \frac{2}{7}$

2 sevenths is 2 lots of 1 seventh.

| $\frac{1}{7}$ | $\frac{1}{7}$ | $\frac{1}{7}$ | $\frac{1}{7}$ | $\frac{1}{7}$ | $\frac{1}{7}$ | $\frac{1}{7}$ |

4 sevenths is 4 lots of 1 seventh.

| $\frac{1}{7}$ | $\frac{1}{7}$ | $\frac{1}{7}$ | $\frac{1}{7}$ | $\frac{1}{7}$ | $\frac{1}{7}$ | $\frac{1}{7}$ |

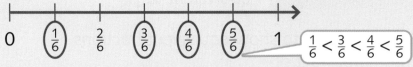

0   $\frac{1}{6}$ $\frac{2}{6}$ $\frac{3}{6}$ $\frac{4}{6}$ $\frac{5}{6}$ 1 $\frac{1}{6} < \frac{3}{6} < \frac{4}{6} < \frac{5}{6}$

When comparing and ordering fractions, if the numerators are all 1 (**unit fractions**), then the greater the denominator, the **smaller** the fraction.

1 eighth is smaller than 1 sixth.
$\frac{1}{8} < \frac{1}{6}$

The denominator represents the number of **equal parts** the **whole** has been **divided into**. The greater this number, the more equal parts and therefore the smaller the size of each part.

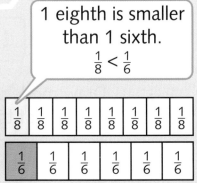

| $\frac{1}{8}$ | $\frac{1}{8}$ | $\frac{1}{8}$ | $\frac{1}{8}$ | $\frac{1}{8}$ | $\frac{1}{8}$ | $\frac{1}{8}$ | $\frac{1}{8}$ |

| $\frac{1}{6}$ | $\frac{1}{6}$ | $\frac{1}{6}$ | $\frac{1}{6}$ | $\frac{1}{6}$ | $\frac{1}{6}$ |

Look at these models and fractions. They all have a numerator of 1.

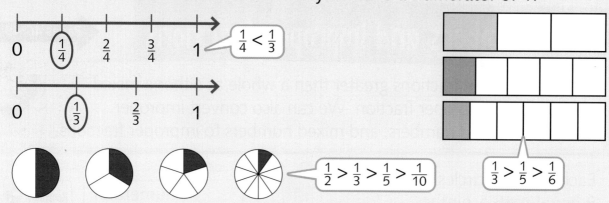

$\frac{1}{4} < \frac{1}{3}$

$\frac{1}{2} > \frac{1}{3} > \frac{1}{5} > \frac{1}{10}$

$\frac{1}{3} > \frac{1}{5} > \frac{1}{6}$

When comparing and ordering fractions, if the numerators are all the same, then the greater the denominator, the smaller the fraction.

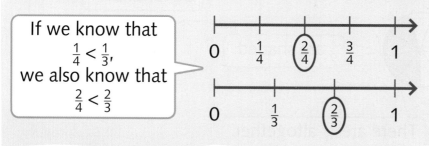

If we know that $\frac{1}{4} < \frac{1}{3}$, we also know that $\frac{2}{4} < \frac{2}{3}$

$\frac{2}{3} > \frac{2}{5} > \frac{2}{6}$

When comparing and ordering fractions, if the denominators are different, we need to convert them to **equivalent fractions** with the same denominator.

Which is greater, $\frac{5}{8}$ or $\frac{3}{4}$?

Find equivalent fractions:

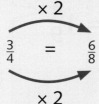

$\frac{3}{4} = \frac{6}{8}$

× 2

× 2

| $\frac{1}{8}$ | $\frac{1}{8}$ | $\frac{1}{8}$ | $\frac{1}{8}$ | $\frac{1}{8}$ | $\frac{1}{8}$ | $\frac{1}{8}$ | $\frac{1}{8}$ |

| $\frac{1}{4}$ | $\frac{1}{4}$ | $\frac{1}{4}$ | $\frac{1}{4}$ |

$\frac{3}{4} > \frac{5}{8}$

 **Draw** **Write** Choose pairs of fractions from different number lines and compare them. Draw models to represent your comparisons.

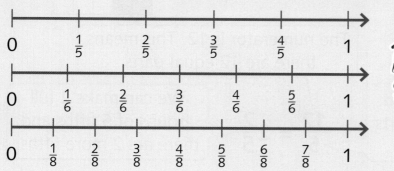

Choose sets of four or five fractions and write them in ascending order.

Pages 50–51

Mixed numbers and improper fractions

Pages 46-49

We can represent fractions greater than a whole as either a mixed number or an improper fraction. We can also convert improper fractions to mixed numbers, and mixed numbers to improper fractions.

Each of these circles is **divided** into 9 **equal parts** – ninths.

Remember

$\dfrac{4}{9}$ — numerator / vinculum / denominator

$\dfrac{9}{9}$ are shaded.

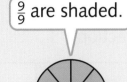

$\dfrac{4}{9}$ are shaded.

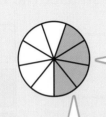

1 **whole** is shaded.

There are $\dfrac{13}{9}$ altogether.

So, $\dfrac{13}{9} = 1$ whole $+ \dfrac{4}{9}$

We say: 13 ninths

1 and 4 ninths

This is called an **improper fraction**. In an improper fraction, the numerator is **greater than**, or **equal to**, the denominator.

$$\dfrac{13}{9} = 1\dfrac{4}{9}$$

This is called a **mixed number**. A mixed number is a number that consists of a **whole number** and a **fraction**.

Converting an improper fraction to a mixed number

Let's look at the improper fraction $\dfrac{12}{5}$.

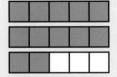

The denominator is 5. This tells us that each whole has been **divided** into 5 equal parts. 5 parts make each whole.

The numerator is 12. This means there are 12 equal parts.

$$\dfrac{12}{5} = 2\dfrac{2}{5}$$

We can make 2 full groups of 5 fifths and there are 2 more fifths.

We can use our understanding of **division** to help us convert an improper fraction to a mixed number.

As each whole has been divided into 5 equal parts, we divide 12 by 5 to convert the improper fraction to a mixed number.

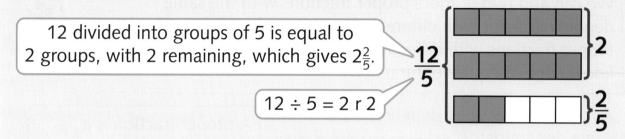

12 divided into groups of 5 is equal to 2 groups, with 2 remaining, which gives $2\frac{2}{5}$.

$12 \div 5 = 2\,r\,2$

$\frac{12}{5}$

$\Big\}2$

$\Big\}\frac{2}{5}$

Converting a mixed number to an improper fraction

Let's look at the mixed number $3\frac{3}{4}$.

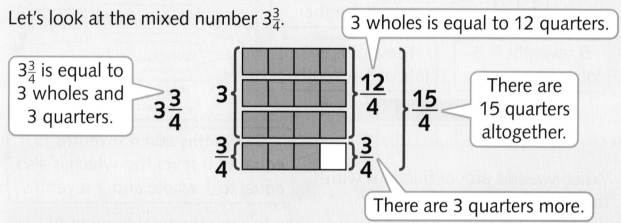

3 wholes is equal to 12 quarters.

$3\frac{3}{4}$ is equal to 3 wholes and 3 quarters.

$3\frac{3}{4}$

$3\Big\{$

$\frac{12}{4}$

$\frac{15}{4}$

There are 15 quarters altogether.

$\frac{3}{4}\Big\{$ $\Big\}\frac{3}{4}$

There are 3 quarters more.

We can use our understanding of **multiplication** and **addition** to help us convert a mixed number to an improper fraction.

There are 3 groups of $\frac{4}{4}$, which is $\frac{12}{4}$
$(3 \times 4 = 12)$

$3\frac{3}{4} = \frac{15}{4}$

$\frac{12}{4} + \frac{3}{4} = \frac{15}{4}$

There are 3 quarters more.
$(12 + 3 = 15)$

 Draw Write

Draw and label bar models to convert each improper fraction to a mixed number, and each mixed number to an improper fraction.

$\frac{11}{5}$ $\frac{23}{6}$ $\frac{21}{4}$ $2\frac{3}{10}$ $5\frac{2}{3}$ $4\frac{5}{8}$

Pages 52–53, 56–59, 62–63, 66–67

Add proper fractions

Pages 26-27, 46-47, 50-51

We can add two or more proper fractions with the same denominators or with different denominators. When we add proper fractions with different denominators, we need to apply our knowledge of equivalent fractions.

Add proper fractions with the same denominator

$\frac{5}{7} + \frac{4}{7} = \boxed{\frac{9}{7}} = \boxed{1\frac{2}{7}}$

Always convert an improper fraction to a mixed number.

A proper fraction is a fraction with a numerator less than its denominator.

$\frac{5}{7}$
numerator
vinculum
denominator

Remember

5 sevenths is 5 lots of 1 seventh.

4 sevenths is 4 lots of 1 seventh.

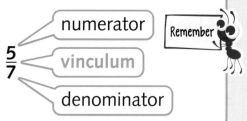

5 sevenths add 4 sevenths is equal to 9 sevenths, which is also equal to 1 whole and 2 sevenths.

When we add proper fractions with the same denominator, the denominators stay the same because they tell you the total number of parts in the whole, and the total number of parts does not change.

We just add the numerators to find out how many parts of the whole there are altogether.

Add proper fractions with different denominators

Unlike fractions are fractions with different denominators. To add them, we first need to convert one or both of the fractions to an equivalent fraction so that both fractions have the same denominator – a common denominator.

$\frac{1}{2} + \frac{1}{8} = \boxed{\frac{5}{8}}$

$\frac{1}{2}$ and $\frac{1}{8}$ are related fractions because the denominator '8' is a multiple of the other denominator '2'.

This bar model has been divided into eighths.

$\frac{1}{2}$ is equivalent to $\frac{4}{8}$.

$\frac{4}{8}$ add $\frac{1}{8}$ is equal to $\frac{5}{8}$.

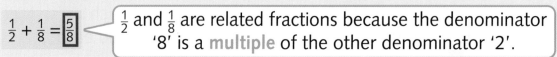

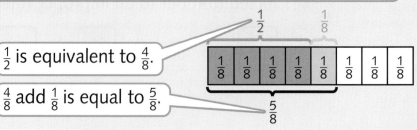

We can work out the answer to this calculation using the following method:

$$\frac{1}{2} + \frac{1}{8} =$$

$$\frac{1}{2} \underset{\times 4}{\overset{\times 4}{=}} \frac{4}{8}$$

> Convert $\frac{1}{2}$ to the equivalent fraction $\frac{4}{8}$.

$$\frac{4}{8} + \frac{1}{8} = \boxed{\frac{5}{8}}$$

We can use the same method when adding non-unit fractions with different denominators.

$$\frac{7}{12} + \frac{5}{6} = \boxed{\frac{17}{12}} = \boxed{1\frac{5}{12}}$$

> Convert $\frac{5}{6}$ to the equivalent fraction $\frac{10}{12}$.

> Convert the improper fraction $\frac{17}{12}$ to the mixed number $1\frac{5}{12}$.

> $\frac{7}{12}$ and $\frac{5}{6}$ are related fractions because the denominator '12' is a multiple of the other denominator '6'.

$$\frac{7}{12} + \frac{5}{6} =$$

$$\frac{5}{6} \underset{\times 2}{\overset{\times 2}{=}} \frac{10}{12}$$

$$\frac{7}{12} + \frac{10}{12} = \boxed{\frac{17}{12}} = \boxed{1\frac{5}{12}}$$

Add three or more proper fractions

We can also use this method when adding three or more proper fractions with different denominators.

$$\frac{3}{4} + \frac{5}{8} + \frac{1}{2} = \boxed{\frac{15}{8}} = \boxed{1\frac{7}{8}}$$

> $\frac{3}{4}$, $\frac{5}{8}$ and $\frac{1}{2}$ are all related fractions because the denominator '8' is a multiple of the other denominators '4' and '2'.

$$\frac{3}{4} + \frac{5}{8} + \frac{1}{2} =$$

> Convert to equivalent fractions: $\frac{3}{4}$ to $\frac{6}{8}$ and $\frac{1}{2}$ to $\frac{4}{8}$.

$$\frac{3}{4} \underset{\times 2}{\overset{\times 2}{=}} \frac{6}{8} \qquad \frac{1}{2} \underset{\times 4}{\overset{\times 4}{=}} \frac{4}{8}$$

$$\frac{6}{8} + \frac{5}{8} + \frac{4}{8} = \boxed{\frac{15}{8}} = \boxed{1\frac{7}{8}}$$

> Convert the improper fraction $\frac{15}{8}$ to the mixed number $1\frac{7}{8}$.

 Draw Write

Draw bar models or use the method above to work out the answers to these fraction addition calculations. Record your answers as mixed numbers.

$$\frac{5}{12} + \frac{2}{3} = \boxed{}$$

$$\frac{1}{3} + \frac{4}{15} = \boxed{}$$

$$\frac{1}{4} + \frac{9}{16} + \frac{3}{8} = \boxed{}$$

Pages 54-57, 60-63

Subtract proper fractions

Pages 26-27, 46-47

We can subtract proper fractions with the same denominators or with different denominators. When we subtract proper fractions with different denominators, we need to apply our knowledge of equivalent fractions.

Subtract proper fractions with the same denominator

$$\frac{7}{12} - \frac{5}{12} = \boxed{\frac{2}{12}}$$

This bar model has been divided into twelfths.

7 twelfths is 7 lots of 1 twelfth.

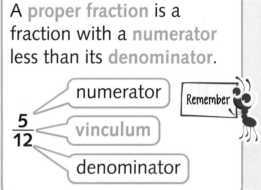

A **proper fraction** is a fraction with a **numerator** less than its **denominator**.

$\frac{5}{12}$ — numerator, vinculum, denominator

Remember

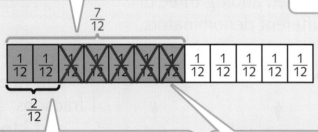

$\frac{7}{12}$

$\frac{2}{12}$

7 twelfths **subtract** 5 twelfths **is equal to** 2 twelfths.

5 twelfths is 5 lots of 1 twelfth.

When we **subtract** proper fractions with the same denominator, the denominators stay the same because they tell you the total number of parts in the **whole**, and the total number of parts does not change.

We just subtract the numerators to find out how many parts of the whole are **left**.

Subtract proper fractions with different denominators

Unlike fractions are fractions with different denominators. To subtract them, we first need to convert one or both of the fractions to an **equivalent fraction** so that both fractions have a **common denominator**.

$$\frac{1}{3} - \frac{1}{9} = \boxed{\frac{2}{9}}$$

$\frac{1}{3}$ and $\frac{1}{9}$ are related fractions because the denominator '9' is a **multiple** of the other denominator '3'.

This model has been divided into ninths.

$\frac{1}{3}$ is equivalent to $\frac{3}{9}$.

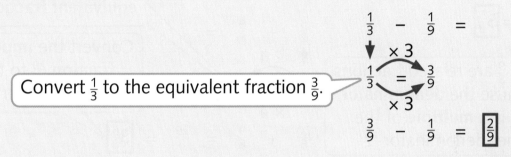

$\frac{3}{9}$ subtract $\frac{1}{9}$ is equal to $\frac{2}{9}$.

We can work out the answer to this calculation using the following method:

$$\frac{1}{3} - \frac{1}{9} = \boxed{}$$

$$\frac{1}{3} \underset{\times 3}{\overset{\times 3}{=}} \frac{3}{9}$$

Convert $\frac{1}{3}$ to the equivalent fraction $\frac{3}{9}$.

$$\frac{3}{9} - \frac{1}{9} = \boxed{\frac{2}{9}}$$

We can use the same method when subtracting non-unit fractions with different denominators.

$$\frac{3}{4} - \frac{5}{16} = \boxed{\frac{7}{16}}$$

$\frac{3}{4}$ and $\frac{5}{16}$ are related fractions because the denominator '16' is a multiple of the other denominator '4'.

$$\frac{3}{4} - \frac{5}{16} =$$

$$\frac{3}{4} \underset{\times 4}{\overset{\times 4}{=}} \frac{12}{16}$$

Convert $\frac{3}{4}$ to the equivalent fraction $\frac{12}{16}$.

$$\frac{12}{16} - \frac{5}{16} = \boxed{\frac{7}{16}}$$

 Draw

 Write

Draw models or use the method above to work out the answers to these fraction subtraction calculations.

$\frac{1}{3} - \frac{1}{12} = \boxed{}$ $\frac{1}{5} - \frac{1}{20} = \boxed{}$

$\frac{3}{4} - \frac{5}{12} = \boxed{}$ $\frac{4}{5} - \frac{7}{15} = \boxed{}$

Pages 58-59

Add mixed numbers

Pages 26-27, 46-47, 50-53

To add two fractions where one or both are mixed numbers or improper fractions, we apply our knowledge of converting between mixed numbers and improper fractions, and of finding equivalent fractions with common denominators.

Add two improper fractions

$$\frac{5}{2} + \frac{9}{8} = \boxed{3\frac{5}{8}}$$

$\frac{5}{2}$ and $\frac{9}{8}$ are related fractions because the denominator '8' is a multiple of the other denominator '2'.

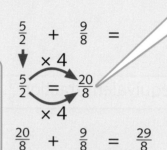

Convert $\frac{5}{2}$ to the equivalent fraction $\frac{20}{8}$.

Convert the improper fraction $\frac{29}{8}$ to the mixed number $3\frac{5}{8}$.

$$\frac{5}{2} \; + \; \frac{9}{8} \; =$$

$$\frac{5}{2} \overset{\times 4}{\underset{\times 4}{=}} \frac{20}{8}$$

$$\frac{20}{8} \; + \; \frac{9}{8} \; = \; \frac{29}{8} \; = \; \boxed{3\frac{5}{8}}$$

How else could you solve this fraction addition?

Add an improper fraction to a mixed number

Method 1: Convert the improper fraction to a mixed number.

$$2\frac{1}{3} + \frac{11}{6} = \boxed{4\frac{1}{6}}$$

11 divided into groups of 6 is equal to 1 group, with 5 remaining, which gives $1\frac{5}{6}$.

$11 \div 6 = 1\ r\ 5$ $\qquad$ $\frac{11}{6} = 1\frac{5}{6}$

Convert $\frac{1}{3}$ to the equivalent fraction $\frac{2}{6}$.

Combine the whole and fraction parts.

$$2\frac{1}{3} \; + \; 1\frac{5}{6} \; =$$

$$\frac{1}{3} \overset{\times 2}{\underset{\times 2}{=}} \frac{2}{6}$$

$$2\frac{2}{6} \; + \; 1\frac{5}{6} \; = \; 3\frac{7}{6} \; = \; \boxed{4\frac{1}{6}}$$

Convert $\frac{7}{6}$ to the mixed number $1\frac{1}{6}$. $(3 + 1\frac{1}{6} = 4\frac{1}{6})$

Method 2: Convert the mixed number to an improper fraction.

There are 2 groups of $\frac{3}{3}$, which is $\frac{6}{3}$. $(2 \times 3 = 6)$

There is 1 third more. $(6 + 1 = 7)$

$$\frac{7}{3} \; + \; \frac{11}{6} \; =$$

Convert $\frac{7}{3}$ to the equivalent fraction $\frac{14}{6}$.

$$\frac{7}{3} \overset{\times 2}{\underset{\times 2}{=}} \frac{14}{6}$$

$$2\frac{1}{3} = \frac{7}{3} \qquad \frac{6}{3} + \frac{1}{3} = \frac{7}{3}$$

$$\frac{14}{6} \; + \; \frac{11}{6} \; = \; \frac{25}{6} \; = \; \boxed{4\frac{1}{6}}$$

Convert the improper fraction to a mixed number.

Add a proper fraction to a mixed number

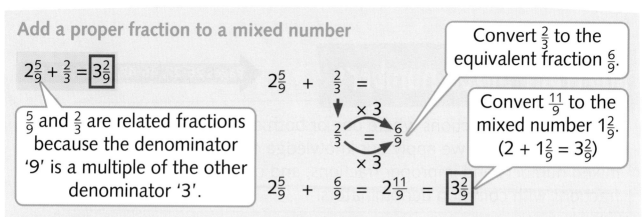

$2\frac{5}{9} + \frac{2}{3} = \boxed{3\frac{2}{9}}$

$\frac{5}{9}$ and $\frac{2}{3}$ are related fractions because the denominator '9' is a multiple of the other denominator '3'.

$2\frac{5}{9} + \frac{2}{3} =$

Convert $\frac{2}{3}$ to the equivalent fraction $\frac{6}{9}$.

$\frac{2}{3} \overset{\times 3}{\underset{\times 3}{=}} \frac{6}{9}$

Convert $\frac{11}{9}$ to the mixed number $1\frac{2}{9}$. $(2 + 1\frac{2}{9} = 3\frac{2}{9})$

$2\frac{5}{9} + \frac{6}{9} = 2\frac{11}{9} = \boxed{3\frac{2}{9}}$

How else could you solve this fraction addition?

Add two mixed numbers

$3\frac{1}{9} + 4\frac{2}{3} = \boxed{7\frac{7}{9}}$

Method 1: Add the whole numbers then add the fractions.

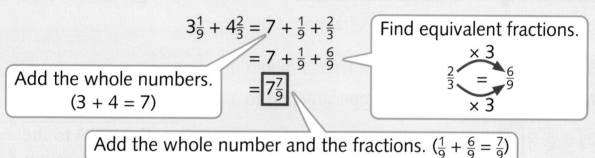

$$3\frac{1}{9} + 4\frac{2}{3} = 7 + \frac{1}{9} + \frac{2}{3}$$
$$= 7 + \frac{1}{9} + \frac{6}{9}$$
$$= \boxed{7\frac{7}{9}}$$

Add the whole numbers. $(3 + 4 = 7)$

Find equivalent fractions.

$\frac{2}{3} \overset{\times 3}{\underset{\times 3}{=}} \frac{6}{9}$

Add the whole number and the fractions. $(\frac{1}{9} + \frac{6}{9} = \frac{7}{9})$

Method 2: Convert both mixed numbers to improper fractions.

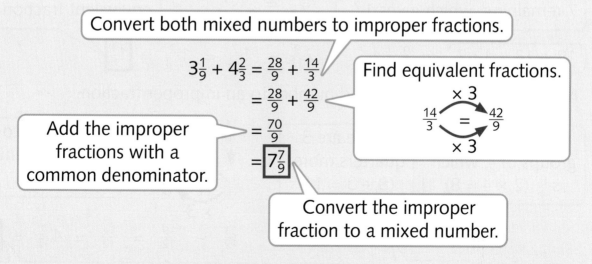

Convert both mixed numbers to improper fractions.

$$3\frac{1}{9} + 4\frac{2}{3} = \frac{28}{9} + \frac{14}{3}$$
$$= \frac{28}{9} + \frac{42}{9}$$
$$= \frac{70}{9}$$
$$= \boxed{7\frac{7}{9}}$$

Find equivalent fractions.

$\frac{14}{3} \overset{\times 3}{\underset{\times 3}{=}} \frac{42}{9}$

Add the improper fractions with a common denominator.

Convert the improper fraction to a mixed number.

Pages 58-59

Subtract mixed numbers

Pages 26-27, 46-47, 50-51, 54-55

To subtract two fractions where one or both are mixed numbers or improper fractions, we apply our knowledge of converting between mixed numbers and improper fractions, and of finding equivalent fractions with common denominators.

Subtract two improper fractions

$\frac{5}{3} - \frac{10}{9} = \boxed{\frac{5}{9}}$

$\frac{5}{3}$ and $\frac{10}{9}$ are related **fractions** because the **denominator** '9' is a **multiple** of the other denominator '3'.

$\frac{5}{3} - \frac{10}{9} =$

$\frac{5}{3} \xrightarrow{\times 3} \frac{15}{9}$ (× 3)

Convert $\frac{5}{3}$ to the **equivalent** fraction $\frac{15}{9}$.

$\frac{15}{9} - \frac{10}{9} = \boxed{\frac{5}{9}}$

How else could you solve this fraction subtraction?

Subtract an improper fraction from a mixed number

Method 1: Convert the improper fraction to a mixed number.

$2\frac{3}{4} - \frac{19}{12} = \boxed{1\frac{1}{6}}$

19 **divided** into groups of 12 **is equal to** 1 group, with 7 remaining, which gives $1\frac{7}{12}$.

$19 \div 12 = 1\ r\ 7$ ⟶ $\frac{19}{12} = 1\frac{7}{12}$

$2\frac{3}{4} - 1\frac{7}{12} =$

$\frac{3}{4} \xrightarrow{\times 3} \frac{9}{12}$ (× 3)

Convert $\frac{3}{4}$ to the equivalent fraction $\frac{9}{12}$.

Reduce $\frac{2}{12}$ to the equivalent fraction $\frac{1}{6}$.

$2\frac{9}{12} - 1\frac{7}{12} = 1\frac{2}{12} = \boxed{1\frac{1}{6}}$

Method 2: Convert the mixed number to an improper fraction.

There are 2 groups of $\frac{4}{4}$, which is $\frac{8}{4}$. (2 × 4 = 8)

There are 3 quarters more. (8 + 3 = 11)

$2\frac{3}{4} = \frac{11}{4}$

$\frac{8}{4} + \frac{3}{4} = \frac{11}{4}$

$\frac{11}{4} - \frac{19}{12} =$

$\frac{11}{4} \xrightarrow{\times 3} \frac{33}{12}$ (× 3)

Convert $\frac{11}{4}$ to the equivalent fraction $\frac{33}{12}$.

$\frac{33}{12} - \frac{19}{12} = \frac{14}{12} = 1\frac{2}{12} = \boxed{1\frac{1}{6}}$

Convert the improper fraction to a mixed number and reduce to an equivalent fraction.

Subtract a proper fraction from a mixed number

$$2\frac{2}{5} - \frac{3}{10} = \boxed{2\frac{1}{10}}$$

$\frac{2}{5}$ and $\frac{3}{10}$ are related fractions because the denominator '10' is a multiple of the other denominator '5'.

$$2\frac{2}{5} \quad - \quad \frac{3}{10} \quad =$$

$$\frac{2}{5} \underset{\times 2}{\overset{\times 2}{=}} \frac{4}{10}$$

Convert $\frac{2}{5}$ to the equivalent fraction $\frac{4}{10}$.

$$2\frac{4}{10} \quad - \quad \frac{3}{10} \quad = \quad \boxed{2\frac{1}{10}}$$

How else could you solve this fraction subtraction?

Subtract two mixed numbers

$$4\frac{1}{3} - 1\frac{7}{12} = \boxed{2\frac{3}{4}}$$

Method 1: Subtract the whole numbers then subtract the fractions.

Find equivalent fractions.

$$\frac{1}{3} \underset{\times 4}{\overset{\times 4}{=}} \frac{4}{12}$$

$$4\frac{1}{3} - 1\frac{7}{12} = 4\frac{4}{12} - 1\frac{7}{12}$$
$$= 3\frac{16}{12} - 1\frac{7}{12}$$
$$= 2\frac{9}{12}$$
$$= \boxed{2\frac{3}{4}}$$

⚠ We can't subtract the fractions because $\frac{4}{12}$ is less than $\frac{7}{12}$. So, **exchange** 1 whole for 12 twelfths. $(4\frac{4}{12} = 3\frac{16}{12})$

Subtract the whole numbers, then subtract the fractions.

Reduce $\frac{9}{12}$ to the equivalent fraction $\frac{3}{4}$.

Method 2: Convert both mixed numbers to improper fractions.

Convert both mixed numbers to improper fractions.

$$4\frac{1}{3} - 1\frac{7}{12} = \frac{13}{3} - \frac{19}{12}$$
$$= \frac{52}{12} - \frac{19}{12}$$
$$= \frac{33}{12}$$
$$= 2\frac{9}{12}$$
$$= \boxed{2\frac{3}{4}}$$

Find equivalent fractions.

$$\frac{13}{3} \underset{\times 4}{\overset{\times 4}{=}} \frac{52}{12}$$

Subtract the improper fractions with a common denominator.

Convert the improper fraction to a mixed number.

Reduce $\frac{9}{12}$ to the equivalent fraction $\frac{3}{4}$.

Multiply a proper fraction by a whole number

Pages 46-47, 52-53

We can use our understanding of multiplication as repeated addition, and of adding proper fractions, to multiply a proper fraction by a whole number.

$\frac{1}{6} \times 5 = \boxed{\frac{5}{6}}$

Look at this model.

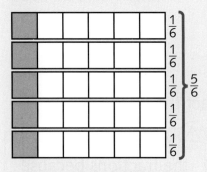

A **proper fraction** is a fraction with a **numerator** less than its **denominator**.

numerator — Remember

$\frac{5}{6}$ — **division bar** or **vinculum**

denominator

There are 5 wholes.

Each **whole** has been **divided into** 6 **equal parts**, and 1 part of each whole is shaded.

There are 5 sixths shaded **altogether**.

We can represent this using this calculation:

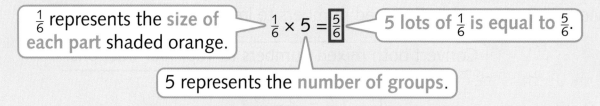

$\frac{1}{6}$ represents the **size of each part** shaded orange.

$\frac{1}{6} \times 5 = \boxed{\frac{5}{6}}$

5 lots of $\frac{1}{6}$ is equal to $\frac{5}{6}$.

5 represents the **number of groups**.

We can represent this on a number line.

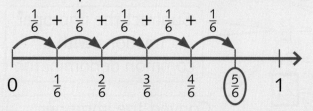

$\frac{1}{6} + \frac{1}{6} + \frac{1}{6} + \frac{1}{6} + \frac{1}{6}$

0   $\frac{1}{6}$ $\frac{2}{6}$ $\frac{3}{6}$ $\frac{4}{6}$ $\left(\frac{5}{6}\right)$ 1

We can think of multiplication as **repeated addition**. — Remember

The calculation above involves multiplying a **unit fraction** ($\frac{1}{6}$) by a **whole number**.

We can also multiply a **non-unit fraction**, such as $\frac{2}{7}$, by a whole number.

$\frac{2}{7} \times 2 = \boxed{\frac{4}{7}}$

Look at this model.

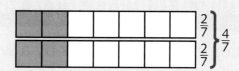

There are 2 wholes.

Each whole has been divided into 7 equal parts, and 2 parts of each whole are shaded.

There are 4 sevenths shaded altogether.

We can represent this using this calculation:

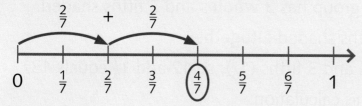

$\frac{2}{7}$ represents the size of each part shaded orange.

$\frac{2}{7} \times 2 = \boxed{\frac{4}{7}}$

2 lots of $\frac{2}{7}$ is equal to $\frac{4}{7}$.

2 represents the number of groups.

We can also represent this on a number line.

$\frac{2}{7}$ + $\frac{2}{7}$

0   $\frac{1}{7}$ $\frac{2}{7}$ $\frac{3}{7}$ $\frac{4}{7}$ $\frac{5}{7}$ $\frac{6}{7}$ 1

Look at the two calculations again.

$\frac{1}{6} \times 5 = \boxed{\frac{5}{6}}$ $\frac{2}{7} \times 2 = \boxed{\frac{4}{7}}$

What's the same? What's different?

Look at the answers. What has happened to the numerator?

What has happened to the denominator?

We can say that when multiplying a proper fraction by a whole number, the numerator of the fraction is multiplied by the whole number, and the denominator stays the same.

Remember Multiplication is **commutative**.

So, $\frac{2}{7} \times 2 = \boxed{\frac{4}{7}}$ and $2 \times \frac{2}{7} = \boxed{\frac{4}{7}}$

Pages 62-63

Multiply a mixed number by a whole number

Pages 46–47, 50–53, 60–61

When we multiply a mixed number by a whole number, we apply our understanding of multiplication as repeated addition and of converting between mixed numbers and improper fractions.

$3\frac{2}{5} \times 4 = \boxed{13\frac{3}{5}}$

Look at this model.

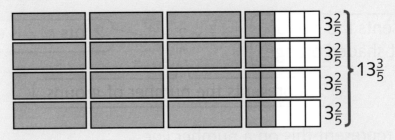

There are 4 groups, and each group has 3 **wholes** and 2 fifths shaded.

There are 12 wholes and 8 fifths shaded **altogether**.

8 fifths ($\frac{8}{5}$) **is equal to** 1 whole and 3 fifths ($1\frac{3}{5}$), so 12 add $1\frac{3}{5}$ equals $13\frac{3}{5}$.

We can represent this using this calculation:

$3\frac{2}{5}$ represents the **size of each part** shaded orange.

$3\frac{2}{5} \times 4 = \boxed{13\frac{3}{5}}$

4 lots of $3\frac{2}{5}$ is equal to $13\frac{3}{5}$.

4 represents the **number of groups**.

We can work out this calculation using different methods.

Method 1: **Repeated addition**.

$3\frac{2}{5} \times 4 = 3\frac{2}{5} + 3\frac{2}{5} + 3\frac{2}{5} + 3\frac{2}{5}$

$= 12\frac{8}{5}$

$= \boxed{13\frac{3}{5}}$

4 lots of $3\frac{2}{5}$ is equal to 4 lots of 3 wholes and 4 lots of $\frac{2}{5}$.

Convert the improper fraction $\frac{8}{5}$ to the mixed number $1\frac{3}{5}$. ($12 + 1\frac{3}{5} = 13\frac{3}{5}$)

Method 2: Partition, then **multiply** the **whole number** and then the **fraction**.

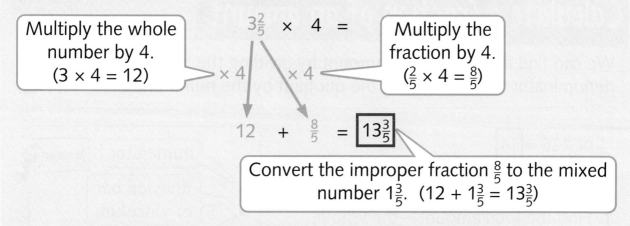

Multiply the whole number by 4.
$(3 \times 4 = 12)$

$3\frac{2}{5} \times 4 =$

Multiply the fraction by 4.
$(\frac{2}{5} \times 4 = \frac{8}{5})$

$\times 4$ $\times 4$

$12 + \frac{8}{5} = \boxed{13\frac{3}{5}}$

Convert the improper fraction $\frac{8}{5}$ to the mixed number $1\frac{3}{5}$. $(12 + 1\frac{3}{5} = 13\frac{3}{5})$

Method 3: Convert the mixed number to an improper fraction.

Convert the mixed number $3\frac{2}{5}$ to the improper fraction $\frac{17}{5}$.

$3\frac{2}{5} \times 4 = \frac{17}{5} \times 4$

$= \frac{68}{5}$

Multiply the improper fraction by the whole number.

Convert the improper fraction $\frac{68}{5}$ to the mixed number $13\frac{3}{5}$.

$= \boxed{13\frac{3}{5}}$

What's similar about each of these three methods?

What's different?

Which method do you prefer? Why?

Multiplication is **commutative**.

So, $3\frac{2}{5} \times 4 = \boxed{13\frac{3}{5}}$ and $4 \times 3\frac{2}{5} = \boxed{13\frac{3}{5}}$

Use your preferred method to work out the answers to these calculations.

$1\frac{1}{4} \times 4 = \boxed{}$ $5 \times 2\frac{1}{3} = \boxed{}$

$3\frac{5}{6} \times 5 = \boxed{}$ $3 \times 4\frac{3}{5} = \boxed{}$

Calculate a fraction of an amount

We can find a fraction of an amount by dividing the whole by the denominator and multiplying the quotient by the numerator.

$\frac{1}{9}$ of 126 = 14

To calculate a **unit** fraction of an amount:

1. Find the total amount – the **whole**.

2. **Divide** the whole by the **denominator**.

We can show this in a model.

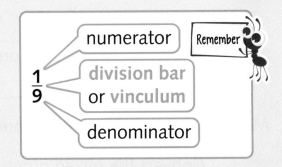

numerator

Remember

$\frac{1}{9}$ division bar or **vinculum**

denominator

126 is the whole.

The whole has been **divided into** 9 **equal groups**.

| 126 |

? — 1 group is 1 ninth of the whole.

When calculating a fraction of an amount, the denominator of the fraction tells us how many equal groups the whole is divided into.

The **numerator** of the fraction tells us **how many groups** of the whole we are finding.

Divide the whole by the denominator. $\frac{1}{9}$ Find the amount in 1 of the groups.

So, to find $\frac{1}{9}$ of 126, divide 126 by 9. — $126 \div 9 = 14$

We can say: — 126 divided into 9 equal groups **is equal to** 14.

We can also say: — 1 ninth of 126 equals 14.

 Draw Draw models to find:

$\frac{1}{6}$ of 96 = ☐ $\frac{1}{4}$ of 280 = ☐ $\frac{1}{8}$ of 560 = ☐

$\frac{5}{9}$ of 126 = $\boxed{70}$

The **quotient** is the answer to a division calculation. 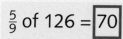 Remember

To calculate a **non-unit** fraction of an amount:

1. Find the total amount – the whole.

2. Divide the whole by the denominator.

3. **Multiply** the quotient by the numerator.

We can show this in a model.

126 is the whole.

126								

The whole has been divided into 9 equal groups.

5 groups is 5 ninths of the whole. ?

 Remember When calculating a fraction of an amount, the denominator of the fraction tells us how many equal groups the whole is divided into.

The numerator of the fraction tells us how many groups of the whole we are finding.

Divide the whole by the denominator. → $\frac{5}{9}$ ← Find the amount in 5 of the groups.

So, to find $\frac{5}{9}$ of 126:

- Divide 126 by 9. ← 126 ÷ 9 = 14

- Then multiply the quotient by 5 to find the answer. ← 14 × 5 = 70

We can say: ← 126 divided into 9 equal groups is equal to 14, and 5 groups of 14 equals 70.

We can also say: ← 5 ninths of 126 is equal to 70.

 Draw Draw models to find:

$\frac{4}{5}$ of 90 = ☐ $\frac{2}{3}$ of 51 = ☐ $\frac{4}{7}$ of 630 = ☐

Tenths, hundredths and thousandths

Decimal numbers are made up of whole numbers and fractions of numbers. A dot, called a decimal point, separates the whole number from the fraction.

Tenths and **hundredths**

This 100 square represents 1 **whole**. It has been divided into 100 **equal parts**.

Each row (or column) is 1 out of 10 equal rows (or columns). This row is 1 **tenth**. As a **fraction**, we write this as $\frac{1}{10}$. As a **decimal**, we write this as 0·1.

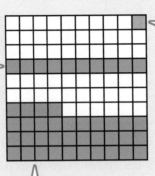

Each square is 1 out of 100 equal squares. This square is 1 **hundredth**. As a fraction, we write this as $\frac{1}{100}$. As a decimal, we write this as 0·01.

There are 34 green squares. So, 34 **hundredths** are shaded green. As a fraction, we write this as $\frac{34}{100}$. As a decimal, we write this as 0·34.

whole number

part of the whole (fractional part) – **tenths**

0·34

part of the whole (fractional part) – hundredths

decimal point

We say: 34 **hundredths**

or zero point three four

Look at these decimals represented using place value grids and part-whole models.

4 **ones** + 2 **tenths** + 3 hundredths = 4·23
4 + 0·2 + 0·03 = 4·23

3 **ones** + 5 **tenths** = 3·5
3 + 0·5 = 3·5

As a fraction we write: $3\frac{5}{10}$

As a fraction we write: $4\frac{23}{100}$

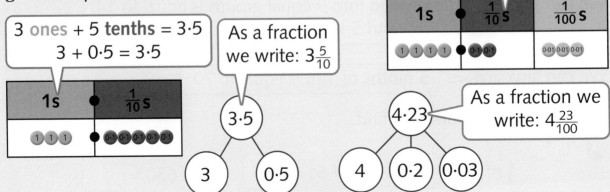

We can position **tenths** on a number line.

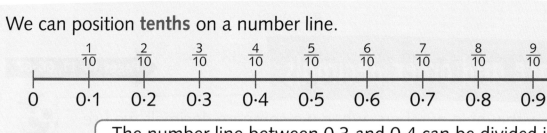

> The number line between 0·3 and 0·4 can be divided into 10 equal parts. Each of these 10 equal parts is one hundredth: $\frac{1}{100}$.

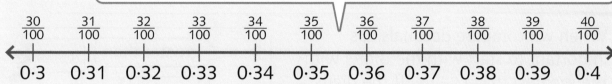

Thousandths

> The number line between 0·33 and 0·34 can be divided into 10 equal parts. Each of these 10 equal parts is one thousandth: $\frac{1}{1,000}$.

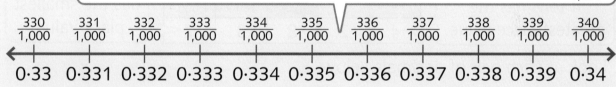

Look at the relationship between **tenths**, hundredths and thousandths.

| 1 is 10 times the size of 1 **tenth**. | 1 **tenth** is 10 times the size of 1 hundredth. | 1 hundredth is 10 times the size of 1 thousandth. |

$$1 = 10 \times \tfrac{1}{10} = \tfrac{10}{10} \qquad \tfrac{1}{10} = 10 \times \tfrac{1}{100} = \tfrac{10}{100} \qquad \tfrac{1}{100} = 10 \times \tfrac{1}{1,000} = \tfrac{10}{1,000}$$

We can represent thousandths using a place value grid and a part-whole model.

> 4 ones + 3 **tenths** + 1 hundredth + 2 thousandths = 4·312
> 4 + 0·3 + 0·01 + 0·002 = 4·312

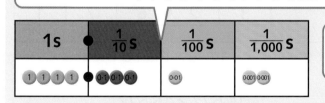

As a fraction we write: $4\frac{312}{1,000}$

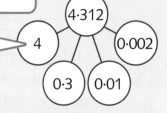

 Draw Draw a place value grid, place value counters or a part-whole model to represent each of these decimals.

 Write For each decimal, what is the value of each digit?

| 0·354 | 4·278 | 21·69 | 14·802 |

Pages 68–93

Compare and order decimals

Pages 10-11, 66-67

Just like with whole numbers, when we compare decimals we use language such as greater/smaller than, and more/less than and the inequality symbols > and <.

When we **compare** decimals, it's important to start with the **digits** with the **greatest place value**. If the digits with the greatest place value are the same, we look at the place value columns to the right until they are different digits.

> — greater than

Remember

< — less than

4 **tens** has the greatest place value.

10s	1s	$\frac{1}{10}$ s	$\frac{1}{100}$ s	$\frac{1}{1,000}$ s
4	2	8	3	7

7 **thousandths** has the smallest place value.

Look at each pair of decimals below.

Compare the digits in place value columns from left to right.

- Start by comparing the **whole numbers**.
- If the whole numbers are the same, compare the **values** of the digits in the **tenths** place.
- If the **tenths** are the same, compare the values of the digits in the **hundredths** place.
- If the **hundredths** are the same, compare the values of the digits in the **thousandths** place.

5 **tenths** are less than 6 **tenths**

32·548 is less than 32·671

32·548 < 32·671

10s	1s	$\frac{1}{10}$ s	$\frac{1}{100}$ s	$\frac{1}{1,000}$ s
3	2	5	4	8
3	2	6	7	1

8 **hundredths** are greater than 6 **hundredths**

54·382 is greater than 54·369

54·382 > 54·369

10s	1s	$\frac{1}{10}$ s	$\frac{1}{100}$ s	$\frac{1}{1,000}$ s
5	4	3	8	2
5	4	3	6	9

7 **thousandths** are less than 8 **thousandths**

16·527 is less than 16·528

16·527 < 16·528

10s	1s	$\frac{1}{10}$ s	$\frac{1}{100}$ s	$\frac{1}{1,000}$ s
1	6	5	2	7
1	6	5	2	8

We can **order** a set of decimal numbers:

in **ascending** order – from **smallest** to **largest/greatest**

or in **descending** order – from largest/greatest to smallest.

Like when we compare decimals, when we order decimals, we start with the digits with the greatest place value. If the digits with the greatest place value are the same, we look at the place value columns to the right until they are different digits.

Descending order – largest to smallest

> If the whole numbers are the same, compare the values of the digits in the **tenths** place.

> Start by comparing whole numbers.

10s	1s	$\frac{1}{10}$s	$\frac{1}{100}$s	$\frac{1}{1,000}$s
2	3	6	0	7
	5	8	3	2
2	5	4	6	
2	3	6	2	
	5	8	3	1

> If the **tenths** are the same, compare the values of the digits in the **hundredths** place.

> If the **hundredths** are the same, compare the values of the digits in the **thousandths** place.

$25.46 > 23.62 > 23.607 > 5.832 > 5.831$

Ascending order – smallest to largest

| 36·045 | < | 36·054 | < | 36·12 | < | 36·153 | < | 36·155 |

1·742   1·744 1·745   1·747   1·749

1·74   1·75

 Write Place each set of numbers in descending order.

12·564   12·6   12·504
12·064   12·561

52·34   52·338   52·4
52·336   52·306

Pages 88–89

Round decimals

Pages 12–13, 66–67

Rounding means changing a number to another number that is close to it in value. Rounding numbers often makes them easier to use. We round decimals in the same way as we round whole numbers.

Round decimals to the nearest whole number

We **round** decimals to the nearest **whole number**, depending on which whole number the decimal is closer to.

To round decimals to the nearest whole number, look at the **digit** in the **tenths** place value.

We can round **tenths** and hundreds to the nearest whole number.

Look at these two decimals.

| 3·24 | | 3·7 |

A number line is a useful tool to help with rounding.

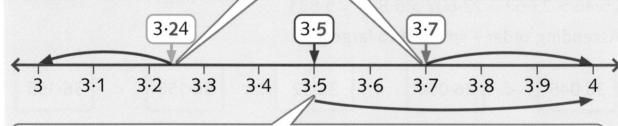

3·24 is closer to 3 than to 4. So, the whole number **stays the same**: 3.

3·7 is closer to 4 than to 3. So, **round up** the whole number to 4.

3·24   3·5   3·7

3   3·1   3·2   3·3   3·4   3·5   3·6   3·7   3·8   3·9   4

Look at the number 3·5. It is exactly **halfway between** 3 and 4. The rule for rounding a number with 5 **tenths** is to round up the whole number.

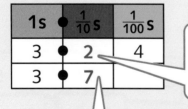

1s	•	$\frac{1}{10}$ s	$\frac{1}{100}$ s
3	•	2	4
3	•	7	

If the value of the **tenths** digit is less than 5, the ones digit stays the same. So, 3·24 rounds to 3.

If the value of the **tenths** digit is 5 or greater, round up the ones digit. So, 3·7 rounds to 4.

Round decimals to the nearest tenth

As well as rounding decimals to the nearest whole number, we can round decimals with **2 decimal places** (hundredths) to the nearest **tenth**.

To round decimals to the nearest **tenth**, look at the digit in the hundredths place value.

Look at these two decimals.

16·43   **16·48**

Once again, a number line is a useful tool to help with rounding.

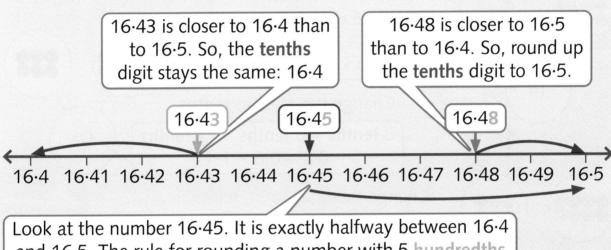

16·43 is closer to 16·4 than to 16·5. So, the **tenths** digit stays the same: 16·4

16·48 is closer to 16·5 than to 16·4. So, round up the **tenths** digit to 16·5.

16·43   16·45   16·48

16·4 16·41 16·42 16·43 16·44 16·45 16·46 16·47 16·48 16·49 16·5

Look at the number 16·45. It is exactly halfway between 16·4 and 16·5. The rule for rounding a number with 5 hundredths is to round up the **tenths**.

10s	1s	$\frac{1}{10}$ s	$\frac{1}{100}$ s
1	6	4	3
1	6	4	8

If the value of the hundredths digit is less than 5, the **tenths** digit stays the same. So, 16·43 rounds to 16·4.

If the value of the hundredths digit is 5 or greater, round up the **tenths** digit. So, 16·48 rounds to 16·5.

Write

Round each of these decimals to the nearest whole number.

Round any decimals with 2 decimal places to the nearest tenth as well.

23·7   **14·26**   **9·73**   **15·2**   **24·08**   **38·5**

Pages 76–79

Use known facts to add decimals

Pages 18-19, 66-67

We can apply place value knowledge to known addition facts to add tenths, hundredths and thousandths.

We can use known facts to help work out addition facts involving **tenths** and hundredths.

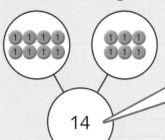

If we know that:
8 ones + 6 ones = 14 ones
8 + 6 = 14
we also know that …

14

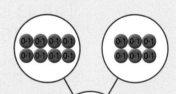

Change the ones to **tenths**.

8 **tenths** + 6 **tenths** = 14 **tenths**
0·8 + 0·6 = 1·4

1·4

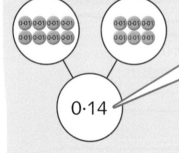

Change the ones to hundredths.

8 hundredths + 6 hundredths = 14 hundredths
0·08 + 0·06 = 0·14

0·14

Addition can be done in any order – it's **commutative**.

Remember

So,

| 8 + 6 = 14 |
| 6 + 8 = 14 |

and

| 0·8 + 0·6 = 1·4 |
| 0·6 + 0·8 = 1·4 |

and

| 0·08 + 0·06 = 0·14 |
| 0·06 + 0·08 = 0·14 |

We can use and apply understanding of **place value** and number facts to **add** different combinations of **tenths**, hundredths and thousandths.

Say How would you calculate each of these additions?

0·06 + 0·78 = ☐   0·07 + 0·5 = ☐

0·57 + 0·006 = ☐   0·35 + 0·9 = ☐   0·3 + 0·008 = ☐

It's also important to recall **complements** that **total 1 whole**.

We can link this with pairs of numbers that total 10, 100 and 1,000.

A 100 square can help us to visualise complements to 1 for **tenths** and hundredths.

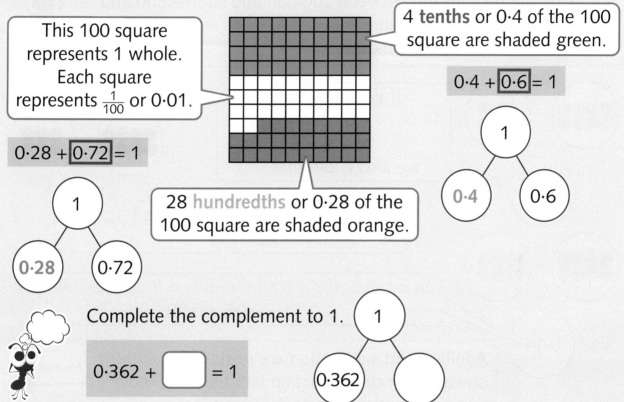

This 100 square represents 1 whole. Each square represents $\frac{1}{100}$ or 0·01.

4 **tenths** or 0·4 of the 100 square are shaded green.

$0·4 + \boxed{0·6} = 1$

$0·28 + \boxed{0·72} = 1$

28 hundredths or 0·28 of the 100 square are shaded orange.

Complete the complement to 1.

$0·362 + \boxed{} = 1$

We can use complements to 1 to help us add pairs of hundredths.

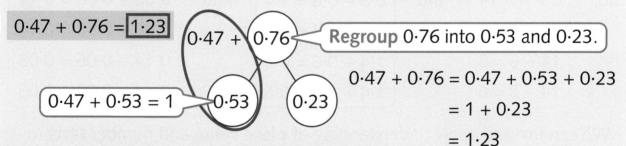

$0·47 + 0·76 = \boxed{1·23}$

$0·47 + 0·76$ — Regroup 0·76 into 0·53 and 0·23.

$0·47 + 0·53 = 1$

$0·47 + 0·76 = 0·47 + 0·53 + 0·23$
$= 1 + 0·23$
$= 1·23$

We can also work this out using a number line.

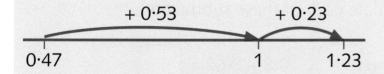

What other methods could you use to work out the answer to 0·46 + 0·76?

Which method do you prefer? Why?

Pages 74-77

Pages 18-19, 66-67, 72-73

Use known facts to subtract decimals

Knowing the relationship between addition and subtraction and being able to apply place value knowledge helps us to subtract tenths, hundredths and thousandths.

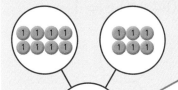

14

If we know that:
14 ones − 6 ones = 8 ones
14 − 6 = 8
we also know that …

1·4

14 tenths − 6 tenths = 8 tenths
1·4 − 0·6 = 0·8

0·14

14 hundredths − 6 hundredths = 8 hundredths
0·14 − 0·06 = 0·08

Remember

Addition and subtraction are related. If we know one addition or subtraction fact then we know three other related facts (**fact families**).

So,

8 + 6 = 14	0·8 + 0·6 = 1·4	0·08 + 0·06 = 0·14
6 + 8 = 14	0·6 + 0·8 = 1·4	0·06 + 0·08 = 0·14
14 − 6 = 8	1·4 − 0·6 = 0·8	0·14 − 0·06 = 0·08
14 − 8 = 6	1·4 − 0·8 = 0·6	0·14 − 0·08 = 0·06

and ... and ...

We can use and apply understanding of **place value** and number facts to **subtract** different combinations of **tenths**, hundredths and thousandths.

Say How would you calculate each of these subtractions?

0·57 − 0·03 = ☐   0·8 − 0·02 = ☐

0·95 − 0·007 = ☐   0·6 − 0·25 = ☐   0·9 − 0·009 = ☐

We can link subtracting pairs of 2-digit numbers to subtracting pairs of decimals with 2 decimal places (hundredths).

$0.42 - 0.25 = \boxed{0.17}$

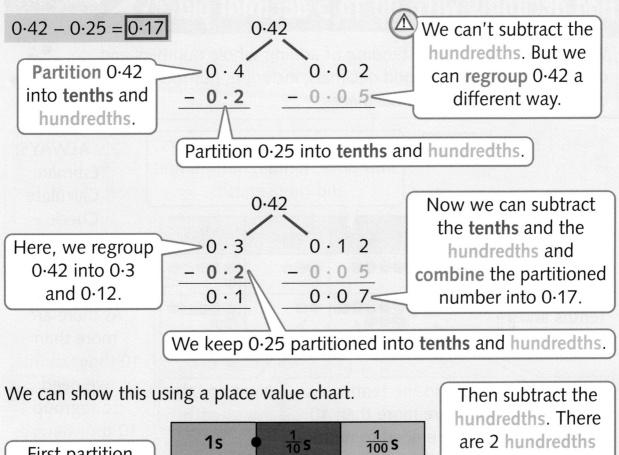

Partition 0·42 into **tenths** and hundredths.

Partition 0·25 into **tenths** and hundredths.

We can't subtract the hundredths. But we can **regroup** 0·42 a different way.

Here, we regroup 0·42 into 0·3 and 0·12.

We keep 0·25 partitioned into **tenths** and hundredths.

Now we can subtract the **tenths** and the hundredths and **combine** the partitioned number into 0·17.

We can show this using a place value chart.

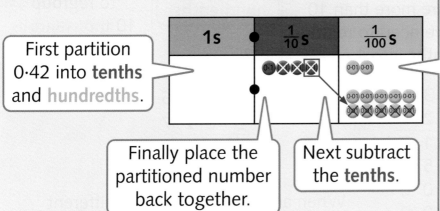

First partition 0·42 into **tenths** and hundredths.

Finally place the partitioned number back together.

Next subtract the **tenths**.

Then subtract the hundredths. There are 2 hundredths in 0·42, and we need to subtract 5 hundredths. As there aren't enough hundredths in 0·42, we need to **exchange** 1 **tenth** for 10 hundredths.

We can also use a number line to work out the answer.

$- 0.05$ $- 0.2$

0·17   0·22   0·42

What other methods could you use to work out the answer to 0·42 – 0·25?

Which method do you prefer? Why?

Pages 78-79

Add decimals with up to 3 decimal places

Pages 20-21, 66-67, 70-73

We can apply our understanding of adding whole numbers and of place value when we add decimals, including numbers with different numbers of decimal places.

$1·436 + 5·827 = \boxed{7·263}$

First **partition** both numbers into ones, **tenths**, hundredths and thousandths.

⚠ **ALWAYS:**
Estimate
Calculate
Check

Finally **combine** the thousandths, hundredths, **tenths** and ones.

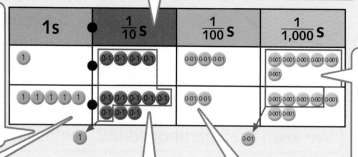

Then **add** the thousandths. As there are more than 10 thousandths, we need to regroup 10 thousandths into 1 hundredth.

Then add the ones.

Now add the **tenths**. As there are more than 10 **tenths**, we need to regroup 10 **tenths** into 1 one.

Next add the hundredths.

We can record this in columns.

```
    1 · 4 3 6
  + 5 · 8 2 7
  ───────────
        1 3
        5 0
    1 · 2 0 0
    6 · 0 0 0
  ───────────
    7 · 2 6 3
```

leads to

```
    1 · 4 3 6
  + 5 · 8 2 7
  ───────────
    7 · 2 6 3
      1     1
```

When adding numbers with different numbers of **decimal places**, it's important to line up the **decimal points** to ensure that each **digit** has the correct **place value**.

$7·8 + 5·64 = \boxed{13·44}$

Add the hundredths.

Add the **tenths**.

Add the ones.

```
      7 · 8
  +   5 · 6 4
  ───────────
      0 · 0 4
      1 · 4 0
    1 2 · 0 0
  ───────────
    1 3 · 4 4
```

leads to

```
      7 · 8
  +   5 · 6 4
  ───────────
    1 3 · 4 4
        1
```

Combine the hundredths, **tenths** and ones.

$3{\cdot}57 + 4{\cdot}864 = \boxed{8{\cdot}434}$

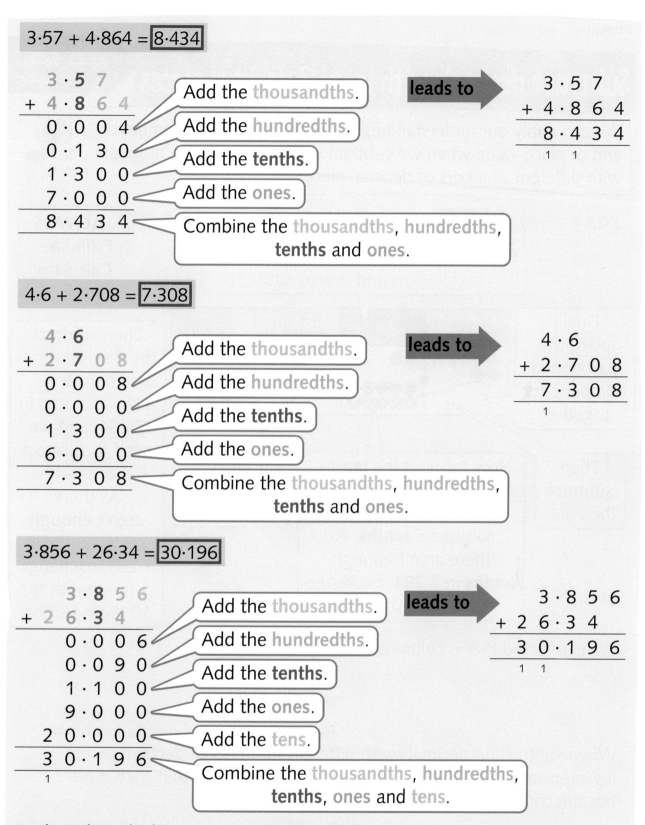

```
  3 · 5 7
+ 4 · 8 6 4
  0 · 0 0 4    Add the thousandths.        leads to    3 · 5 7
  0 · 1 3 0    Add the hundredths.                    + 4 · 8 6 4
  1 · 3 0 0    Add the tenths.                          8 · 4 3 4
  7 · 0 0 0    Add the ones.                              1   1
  8 · 4 3 4    Combine the thousandths, hundredths,
               tenths and ones.
```

$4{\cdot}6 + 2{\cdot}708 = \boxed{7{\cdot}308}$

```
  4 · 6
+ 2 · 7 0 8
  0 · 0 0 8    Add the thousandths.        leads to    4 · 6
  0 · 0 0 0    Add the hundredths.                    + 2 · 7 0 8
  1 · 3 0 0    Add the tenths.                          7 · 3 0 8
  6 · 0 0 0    Add the ones.                              1
  7 · 3 0 8    Combine the thousandths, hundredths,
               tenths and ones.
```

$3{\cdot}856 + 26{\cdot}34 = \boxed{30{\cdot}196}$

```
   3 · 8 5 6
+ 2 6 · 3 4
   0 · 0 0 6    Add the thousandths.       leads to     3 · 8 5 6
   0 · 0 9 0    Add the hundredths.                    + 2 6 · 3 4
   1 · 1 0 0    Add the tenths.                         3 0 · 1 9 6
   9 · 0 0 0    Add the ones.                               1   1
 2 0 · 0 0 0    Add the tens.
 3 0 · 1 9 6    Combine the thousandths, hundredths,
   1            tenths, ones and tens.
```

Look at the calculations on pages 76 and 77.

What other methods could you use to work out the answer to each calculation?

Which method do you prefer? Why?

Subtract decimals with up to 3 decimal places

Pages 22-23, 66-67, 70-71, 74-75

We can apply our understanding of subtracting whole numbers and of place value when we subtract decimals, including numbers with different numbers of decimal places.

$7{\cdot}284 - 3{\cdot}516 = \boxed{3{\cdot}768}$

⚠ **ALWAYS:**
Estimate
Calculate
Check

First **partition** $7{\cdot}284$ into **ones**, **tenths**, **hundredths** and **thousandths**.

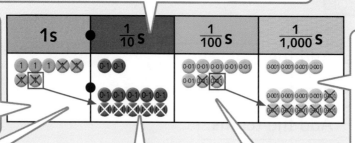

Finally place the partitioned number back together.

Then subtract the **ones**.

Now subtract the **tenths**. There are 2 **tenths** in $7{\cdot}284$, and we need to subtract 5 **tenths**. As there aren't enough **tenths** in $7{\cdot}284$, exchange 1 **one** for 10 **tenths**.

Next subtract the **hundredths**.

Then **subtract** the **thousandths**. There are 4 **thousandths** in $7{\cdot}284$, and we need to subtract 6 **thousandths**. As there aren't enough **thousandths** in $7{\cdot}284$, **exchange** 1 **hundredth** for 10 **thousandths**.

We can record this in columns.

$$\begin{array}{r} {}^{6}\!\!\!\not{7} \cdot {}^{12}\!\!\!\not{2}\ {}^{7}\!\!\!\not{8}\ {}^{14}\!\!\!\not{4} \\ -\ 3 \cdot 5\ \ 1\ \ 6 \\ \hline 3 \cdot 7\ \ 6\ \ 8 \end{array}$$

When subtracting decimals with different numbers of **decimal places**, it's important to line up the **decimal points** to ensure that each **digit** has the correct **place value**.

$6{\cdot}43 - 2{\cdot}8 = \boxed{3{\cdot}63}$

$$\begin{array}{r} {}^{5}\!\!\!\not{6} \cdot {}^{14}\!\!\!\not{4}\ 3 \\ -\ 2 \cdot 8 \\ \hline 3 \cdot 6\ 3 \end{array}$$

There are 4 **tenths** in $6{\cdot}43$, and we need to subtract 8 **tenths**. As there aren't enough **tenths** in $6{\cdot}43$, exchange 1 **one** for 10 **tenths**.

$3 \cdot 2 - 1 \cdot 64 = \boxed{1 \cdot 56}$

$$\begin{array}{r} \overset{2}{\cancel{3}} \cdot \overset{\overset{11}{}\overset{10}{}}{\cancel{2}} \\ - \ 1 \cdot 6 \ 4 \\ \hline 1 \cdot 5 \ 6 \end{array}$$

There are no hundredths in 3·2, and we need to subtract 4 hundredths. As there are no hundredths in 3·2, exchange 1 **tenth** for 10 hundredths.

After the exchange of 1 **tenth** for 10 hundredths there is now 1 **tenth**, and we need to subtract 6 **tenths**. As there aren't enough **tenths**, exchange 1 one for 10 **tenths**.

$12 \cdot 62 - 5 \cdot 736 = \boxed{6 \cdot 884}$

$$\begin{array}{r} \cancel{1}\ \overset{11}{\cancel{2}} \cdot \overset{15}{\cancel{6}}\ \overset{11}{\cancel{2}}\ \overset{10}{} \\ - \quad 5 \cdot 7 \ 3 \ 6 \\ \hline 6 \cdot 8 \ 8 \ 4 \end{array}$$

There are no thousandths in 12·62, and we need to subtract 6 thousandths. As there are no thousandths in 12·62, exchange 1 hundredth for 10 thousandths.

After the exchange of 1 hundredth for 10 thousandths there is now 1 hundredth, and we need to subtract 3 hundredths. As there aren't enough hundredths, exchange 1 **tenth** for 10 hundredths.

There are 2 ones in 12·62, and we need to subtract 5 ones. As there aren't enough ones in 12·62, exchange 1 ten for 10 ones.

$19 \cdot 7 - 8 \cdot 325 = \boxed{11 \cdot 375}$

$$\begin{array}{r} 1 \ 9 \cdot \overset{\overset{9}{}\overset{6\ \ 10}{}\ \ 10}{\cancel{7}} \\ - \quad 8 \cdot 3 \ 2 \ 5 \\ \hline 1 \ 1 \cdot 3 \ 7 \ 5 \end{array}$$

There are no thousandths in 19·7, and we need to subtract 5 thousandths. As there are no hundredths in 19·7, we can't exchange 1 hundredth for 10 thousandths. So we need to exchange 1 **tenth** for 10 hundredths, and then exchange 1 hundredth for 10 thousandths.

After the exchange of 1 **tenth** for 10 hundredths, and the exchange of 1 hundredth for 10 thousandths, there are now 6 **tenths** and 9 hundredths.

Look at the calculations on pages 78 and 79.

What other methods could you use to work out the answer to each calculation?

Which method do you prefer? Why?

Multiply decimals by 10, 100 and 1,000

Pages 30-31, 66-67

It's important to understand what happens to the place value of the digits when you multiply a decimal by 10, 100 or 1,000.

When you move up one row on a Gattegno chart, the number becomes **10 times greater**.

When you move up two rows on a Gattegno chart, the number becomes **100 times greater**.

When you move up three rows on a Gattegno chart, the number becomes **1,000 times greater**.

100	200	300	400	500	600	700	800	900
10	20	30	40	50	60	70	80	90
1	2	3	4	5	6	7	8	9
0·1	0·2	0·3	0·4	0·5	0·6	0·7	0·8	0·9
0·01	0·02	0·03	0·04	0·05	0·06	0·07	0·08	0·09
0·001	0·002	0·003	0·004	0·005	0·006	0·007	0·008	0·009

$0.2 \times 10 = 2$

$0.5 \times 100 = 50$

$0.8 \times 1{,}000 = 800$

Multiplying by 10

When we **multiply** a **decimal** by 10, the value of each **digit** in the number becomes 10 times greater and the digits move one **place value** to the left.

10s	1s •	$\frac{1}{10}$ s	$\frac{1}{100}$ s	$\frac{1}{1,000}$s
	3 •	1	0	2
3	1 •	0	2	

$3.102 \times 10 = 31.02$

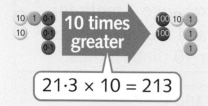

10 times greater

$21.3 \times 10 = 213$

10	20	30	40	50	60	70	80	90
1	2	3	4	5	6	7	8	9
0·1	0·2	0·3	0·4	0·5	0·6	0·7	0·8	0·9
0·01	0·02	0·03	0·04	0·05	0·06	0·07	0·08	0·09

$2.68 \times 10 = 26.8$

100s	10s	1s •	$\frac{1}{10}$ s	$\frac{1}{100}$ s	$\frac{1}{1,000}$s
	2	7 •	9	5	
2	7	9 •	5		

$27.95 \times 10 = 279.5$

Multiplying by 100

When we multiply a decimal by 100, the value of each digit in the number becomes 100 times greater and the digits move two place values to the left. Sometimes we need to include a **zero** to act as a **place holder**.

1,000s	100s	10s	1s	•	$\frac{1}{10}$s	$\frac{1}{100}$s	$\frac{1}{1,000}$s
		8	6	• 5	0	7	
8	6	5	0	• 7			

$$86 \cdot 507 \times 100 = 8,650 \cdot 7$$

100	200	300	400	500	600	700	800	900
10	20	30	40	50	60	70	80	90
1	2	3	4	5	6	7	8	9
0·1	0·2	0·3	0·4	0·5	0·6	0·7	0·8	0·9
0·01	0·02	0·03	0·04	0·05	0·06	0·07	0·08	0·09

$$2 \cdot 69 \times 100 = 269$$

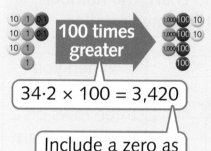

100 times greater

$$34 \cdot 2 \times 100 = 3,420$$

Include a zero as a place holder.

1,000s	100s	10s	1s	•	$\frac{1}{10}$s	$\frac{1}{100}$s	$\frac{1}{1,000}$s
		1	8	• 4	5		
1	8	4	5	•			

$$18 \cdot 45 \times 100 = 1,845$$

Multiplying by 1,000

When we multiply a decimal by 1,000, the value of each digit in the number becomes 1,000 times greater and the digits move three place values to the left. Sometimes we need to include zeros to act as place holders.

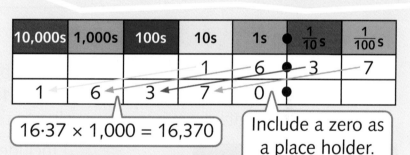

10,000s	1,000s	100s	10s	1s	•	$\frac{1}{10}$s	$\frac{1}{100}$s
			1	6	• 3	7	
1	6	3	7	0	•		

$$16 \cdot 37 \times 1,000 = 16,370$$

Include a zero as a place holder.

1,000	2,000	3,000	4,000	5,000	6,000	7,000	8,000	9,000
100	200	300	400	500	600	700	800	900
10	20	30	40	50	60	70	80	90
1	2	3	4	5	6	7	8	9
0·1	0·2	0·3	0·4	0·5	0·6	0·7	0·8	0·9
0·01	0·02	0·03	0·04	0·05	0·06	0·07	0·08	0·09

$$3 \cdot 58 \times 1,000 = 3,580$$

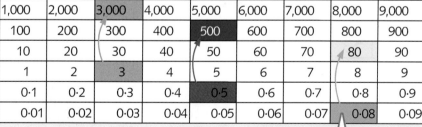

1,000 times greater

$$4 \cdot 3 \times 1,000 = 4,300$$

Include two zeros as place holders.

1,000s	100s	10s	1s	•	$\frac{1}{10}$s	$\frac{1}{100}$s	$\frac{1}{1,000}$s
			2	• 4	7	9	
2	4	7	9	•			

$$2 \cdot 479 \times 1,000 = 2,479$$

Pages 82–85

Divide whole numbers and decimals by 10, 100 and 1,000

Pages 32–33, 66–67, 80–81

It's important to understand what happens to the place value of the digits when you divide whole numbers and decimals by 10, 100 or 1,000.

When you move down one row on a Gattegno chart, the number becomes **10 times smaller**.

When you move down two rows on a Gattegno chart, the number becomes **100 times smaller**.

When you move down three rows on a Gattegno chart, the number becomes **1,000 times smaller**.

100	200	300	400	500	600	700	800	900
10	20	30	40	50	60	70	80	90
1	2	3	4	5	6	7	8	9
0·1	0·2	0·3	0·4	0·5	0·6	0·7	0·8	0·9
0·01	0·02	0·03	0·04	0·05	0·06	0·07	0·08	0·09
0·001	0·002	0·003	0·004	0·005	0·006	0·007	0·008	0·009

$0·2 \div 10 = 0·02$

$0·6 \div 100 = 0·006$

$8 \div 1,000 = 0·008$

Dividing by 10

When we **divide** a **whole number** or a **decimal** by 10, the value of each **digit** in the number becomes 10 times smaller and the digits move one **place value** to the right.

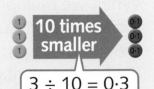

10 times smaller

$3 \div 10 = 0·3$

Include a **zero** as a **place holder**.

100s	10s	1s •	$\frac{1}{10}$s
3	6	5 •	
	3	6 •	5

$365 \div 10 = 36·5$

1	2	3	4	5	6	7	8	9
0·1	0·2	0·3	0·4	0·5	0·6	0·7	0·8	0·9
0·01	0·02	0·03	0·04	0·05	0·06	0·07	0·08	0·09

$6·8 \div 10 = 0·68$

1s •	$\frac{1}{10}$s	$\frac{1}{100}$s	$\frac{1}{1,000}$s
7 •	4	5	
0 •	7	4	5

$7·45 \div 10 = 0·745$

Include a zero as a place holder.

10 times smaller

$42 \div 10 = 4·2$

10	20	30	40	50	60	70	80	90
1	2	3	4	5	6	7	8	9
0·1	0·2	0·3	0·4	0·5	0·6	0·7	0·8	0·9
0·01	0·02	0·03	0·04	0·05	0·06	0·07	0·08	0·09
0·001	0·002	0·003	0·004	0·005	0·006	0·007	0·008	0·009

$14·69 \div 10 = 1·469$

Dividing by 100

When we divide a whole number or a decimal by 100, the value of each digit in the number becomes 100 times smaller and the digits move two place values to the right.

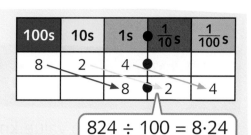

100s	10s	1s	•	$\frac{1}{10}$ s	$\frac{1}{100}$ s
8	2	4			
			8	2	4

824 ÷ 100 = 8·24

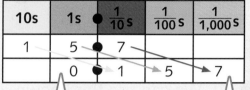

10s	1s	•	$\frac{1}{10}$ s	$\frac{1}{100}$ s	$\frac{1}{1,000}$ s
1	5		7		
	0		1	5	7

1	2	3	4	5	6	7	8	9
0·1	0·2	0·3	0·4	0·5	0·6	0·7	0·8	0·9
0·01	0·02	0·03	0·04	0·05	0·06	0·07	0·08	0·09
0·001	0·002	0·003	0·004	0·005	0·006	0·007	0·008	0·009

Include a zero as a place holder.

15·7 ÷ 100 = 0·157

4·6 ÷ 100 = 0·046

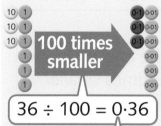

100 times smaller

36 ÷ 100 = 0·36

Include a zero as a place holder.

100	200	300	400	500	600	700	800	900
10	20	30	40	50	60	70	80	90
1	2	3	4	5	6	7	8	9
0·1	0·2	0·3	0·4	0·5	0·6	0·7	0·8	0·9
0·01	0·02	0·03	0·04	0·05	0·06	0·07	0·08	0·09
0·001	0·002	0·003	0·004	0·005	0·006	0·007	0·008	0·009

257·9 ÷ 100 = 2·579

Dividing by 1,000

When we divide a whole number by 1,000, the value of each digit in the number becomes 1,000 times smaller and the digits move three place values to the right.

1,000 times smaller

21 ÷ 1,000 = 0·021

Include two zeros as place holders.

1,000s	100s	10s	1s	•	$\frac{1}{10}$ s	$\frac{1}{100}$ s	$\frac{1}{1,000}$ s
1	5	9	6				
			1		5	9	6

1,596 ÷ 1,000 = 1·596

100	200	300	400	500	600	700	800	900
10	20	30	40	50	60	70	80	90
1	2	3	4	5	6	7	8	9
0·1	0·2	0·3	0·4	0·5	0·6	0·7	0·8	0·9
0·01	0·02	0·03	0·04	0·05	0·06	0·07	0·08	0·09
0·001	0·002	0·003	0·004	0·005	0·006	0·007	0·008	0·009

368 ÷ 1,000 = 0·368

Pages 86-87

Use known facts to multiply decimals

Pages 24–25, 66–67, 80–81

We can apply place value knowledge to known multiplication tables facts to multiply tenths and hundredths.

We can **scale** known multiplication tables facts by 1 **tenth**.

We know that $3 \times 4 = 12$

10 times smaller

We can use this known fact to work out that 3×4 **tenths** = 12 **tenths**
$3 \times 0{\cdot}4 = 1{\cdot}2$

Since one of the numbers in the calculation is 10 times smaller …

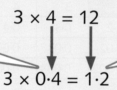
$3 \times 4 = 12$
$3 \times 0{\cdot}4 = 1{\cdot}2$

… the answer is also 10 times smaller.

We know that $3 \times 4 = 12$. We can also use this known fact to work out that
3 **tenths** $\times 4 = 12$ **tenths**
$0{\cdot}3 \times 4 = 1{\cdot}2$

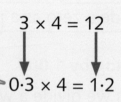
$3 \times 4 = 12$
$0{\cdot}3 \times 4 = 1{\cdot}2$

 Remember

factor × factor = product

Multiplication can be done in any order – it's **commutative**.

$3 \times 4 = 12$ $3 \times 4 = 12$
$3 \times 0{\cdot}4 = 1{\cdot}2$ $0{\cdot}3 \times 4 = 1{\cdot}2$

If one factor is 1 **tenth** of the size, then the product will be 1 **tenth** of the size.

So,

| $3 \times 4 = 12$ | and | $3 \times 0{\cdot}4 = 1{\cdot}2$ | and | $0{\cdot}3 \times 4 = 1{\cdot}2$ |
| $4 \times 3 = 12$ | | $0{\cdot}4 \times 3 = 1{\cdot}2$ | | $4 \times 0{\cdot}3 = 1{\cdot}2$ |

We can also scale known multiplication tables facts by 1 hundredth.

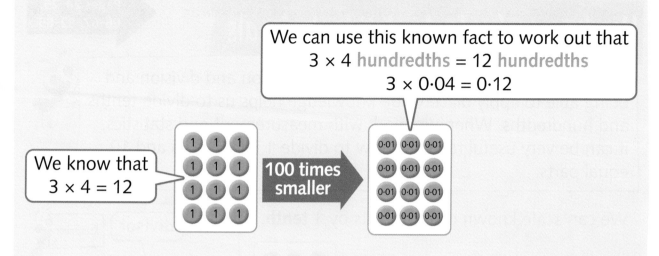

We can use this known fact to work out that
3 × 4 hundredths = 12 hundredths
3 × 0·04 = 0·12

We know that
3 × 4 = 12

100 times smaller

Since one of the numbers in the calculation is 100 times smaller …

3 × 4 = 12

… the answer is also 100 times smaller.

3 × 0·04 = 0·12

We know that 3 × 4 = 12. We can also use this known fact to work out that
3 hundredths × 4 = 12 hundredths
0·03 × 4 = 0·12

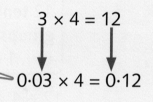

3 × 4 = 12

0·03 × 4 = 0·12

3 × 4 = 12
3 × 0·04 = 0·12

3 × 4 = 12
0·03 × 4 = 0·12

If one factor is 1 hundredth of the size, then the product will be 1 hundredth of the size.

So,

3 × 4 = 12
4 × 3 = 12

and

3 × 0·04 = 0·12
0·04 × 3 = 0·12

and

0·03 × 4 = 0·12
4 × 0·03 = 0·12

Pages 86-87

Use known facts to divide decimals

Pages 24-25, 66-67, 82-85

Knowing the relationship between multiplication and division and being able to apply place value knowledge helps us to divide tenths and hundredths. When we work with measurement and statistics, it can be very useful to know how to divide 1 into 2, 4, 5 and 10 equal parts.

We can **scale** known division facts by 1 **tenth**.

We know that
$12 \div 4 = 3$

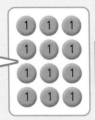

10 times smaller

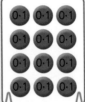

divisor — Remember

$12 \div 4 = \boxed{3}$

dividend   **quotient**

There are 12 **tenths**.
12 **tenths** divided into groups of 4 **tenths** = 3
$1·2 \div 0·4 = 3$

We can also see:
12 **tenths** divided into 4 equal parts = 3 **tenths**
$1·2 \div 4 = 0·3$

$12 \div 4 = 3$

$1·2 \div 0·4 = 3$

$12 \div 4 = 3$

$1·2 \div 4 = 0·3$

If the dividend is 1 **tenth** of the size and the divisor is 1 **tenth** of the size, the quotient remains the same.

If the dividend is 1 **tenth** of the size and the divisor is the same, the quotient is 1 **tenth** of the size.

 Remember · Multiplication and division are related. If we know one multiplication or division fact, we know three other related facts.

So,

$3 \times 4 = 12$	$3 \times 0·4 = 1·2$	$0·3 \times 4 = 1·2$
$4 \times 3 = 12$	$0·4 \times 3 = 1·2$	$4 \times 0·3 = 1·2$
$12 \div 4 = 3$	$1·2 \div 0·4 = 3$	$1·2 \div 4 = 0·3$
$12 \div 3 = 4$	$1·2 \div 3 = 0·4$	$1·2 \div 0·3 = 4$

and   and

We can also scale known division facts by 1 hundredth.

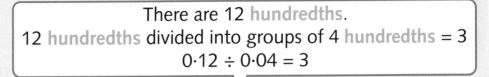
There are 12 hundredths.
12 hundredths divided into groups of 4 hundredths = 3
0·12 ÷ 0·04 = 3

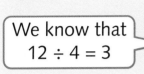
We know that
12 ÷ 4 = 3

100 times smaller

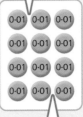

We can also see:
12 hundredths divided into 4 equal parts = 3 hundredths
0·12 ÷ 4 = 0·03

12 ÷ 4 = 3
0·12 ÷ 0·04 = 3

12 ÷ 4 = 3
0·12 ÷ 4 = 0·03

If the dividend is 1 hundredth of the size and the divisor is 1 hundredth of the size, the quotient remains the same.

If the dividend is 1 hundredth of the size and the divisor is the same, the quotient is 1 hundredth of the size.

So,

3 × 4 = 12	3 × 0·04 = 0·12	0·03 × 4 = 0·12
4 × 3 = 12	0·04 × 3 = 0·12	4 × 0·03 = 0·12
12 ÷ 4 = 3	0·12 ÷ 0·04 = 3	0·12 ÷ 4 = 0·03
12 ÷ 3 = 4	0·12 ÷ 3 = 0·04	0·12 ÷ 0·03 = 4

and ... and

It is also important to be able to divide 1 into 2, 4, 5 and 10 equal parts as this is useful when reading and interpreting measuring instruments and graph scales.

1	
0·5	0·5

1			
0·25	0·25	0·25	0·25

1				
0·2	0·2	0·2	0·2	0·2

1									
0·1	0·1	0·1	0·1	0·1	0·1	0·1	0·1	0·1	0·1

Percentages

Pages 66-69

Per cent means per hundred. It represents the number of parts in every 100.

Percentages are like fractions. They tell us the number of parts in every hundred or the number of parts per hundred.

The sign for per cent is %.

We see percentages in everyday life.

20% tells us the amount of money we will save on an item we may want to buy.

We also see percentages on mobiles, tablets and computers.

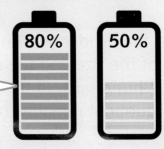

These percentages show us how much battery charge is left.

We can use percentages to compare and order amounts.

These labels tell us the percentages of different fabrics in the clothes.

80% is more than 20%. So, the label tells us that there is more cotton than polyester in this item of clothing.
80% > 20%

This label tells us that this item of clothing consists mostly of viscose.
73% > 22% > 3% > 2%

A percentage is an amount **out of 100**.

100% is the whole amount.

100% is also **equal to** 1.

Look at these 100 squares.

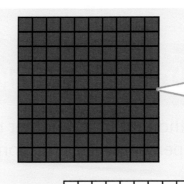

This grid is made up of 100 squares. The whole grid represents 100%.

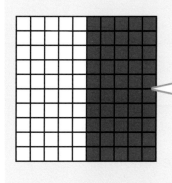

50 parts out of 100 are red. 50% of the grid is red.

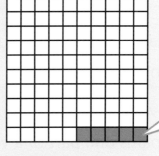

5 parts out of 100 are orange. 5% of the grid is orange.

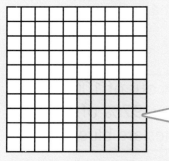

25 parts out of 100 are yellow. 25% of the grid is yellow.

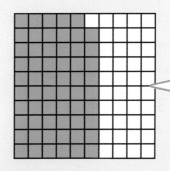

59 parts out of 100 are blue. 59% of the grid is blue.

There are 100 people in the picture. One person is wearing a hat.

We can say that 1% of the people are wearing a hat.

Look at these bar models. Each bar represents 100%.

What per cent does each part of a bar represent?

Use this to work out what per cent of each bar is shaded.

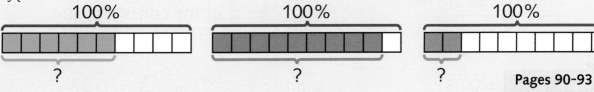

100%
?

100%
?

100%
?

Pages 90-93

Percentages as fractions and decimals

Pages 66-67, 88-89

A percentage can be thought of as another name for hundredths. So, we can represent percentages as fractions with a denominator of 100 or as decimals.

Remember

Percentages tell you the number of **parts in every hundred**.

The sign for **per cent** is %.

Percentages are a way of expressing **proportions**.

A proportion compares one part of a whole with the whole amount.

We can also express proportions as **fractions** and as **decimals**.

In the picture there are 100 cones.

3 **parts out of 100** are red. 3% of the cones are red.

97 parts out of 100 are blue. 97% of the cones are blue.

We can represent these proportions as fractions with **denominators** of 100.

3 cones out of 100 cones are red. $\frac{3}{100}$ of the cones are red.

97 cones out of 100 cones are blue. $\frac{97}{100}$ of the cones are blue.

We can also represent these proportions as **hundredths** expressed as decimals.

3 **hundredths** of the cones are red. 0·03 of the cones are red.

97 **hundredths** of the cones are blue. 0·97 of the cones are blue.

So, $3\% = \frac{3}{100} = 0.03$ and $97\% = \frac{97}{100} = 0.97$

Look at these 100 squares. They are the same 100 squares as the ones on page 89.

We can describe what proportion of each square is shaded as a percentage, as a fraction or as a decimal.

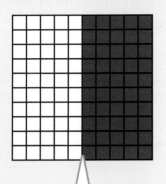

50 parts out of 100 are red.
50% of the grid is red.
$\frac{50}{100}$ of the grid is red.
0·5 of the grid is red.

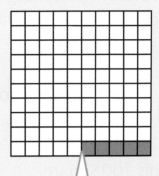

5 parts out of 100 are orange.
5% of the grid is orange.
$\frac{5}{100}$ of the grid is orange.
0·05 of the grid is orange.

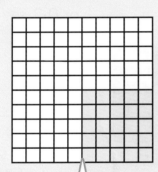

25 parts out of 100 are yellow.
25% of the grid is yellow.
$\frac{25}{100}$ of the grid is yellow.
0·25 of the grid is yellow.

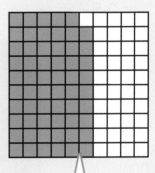

59 parts out of 100 are blue.
59% of the grid is blue.
$\frac{59}{100}$ of the grid is blue.
0·59 of the grid is blue.

What's the same about percentages, fractions and decimals?

What's different?

Look at the red, orange and yellow 100 squares above.

How else could you express what fraction of each square is shaded?

Pages 92-93

Equivalences

Pages 46-47, 66-67, 88-91

We can represent percentages as fractions with a denominator of 100 or as decimals. We can also use percentages to express other fractions and decimals.

 Remember **Percentages** tell you the number of **parts in every hundred**.

The sign for **per cent** is %.

Look at this 100 square.

There are 50 red squares out of 100.
We can write this as 50%.
This is the same as $\frac{50}{100}$, $\frac{5}{10}$, $\frac{1}{2}$ or 0·5.

There are 20 blue squares out of 100.
We can write this as 20%.
This is the same as $\frac{20}{100}$, $\frac{2}{10}$, $\frac{1}{5}$ or 0·2.

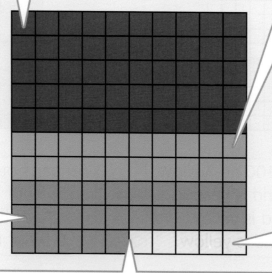

There are 25 green squares out of 100.
We can write this as 25%.
This is the same as $\frac{25}{100}$, $\frac{1}{4}$ or 0·25.

There are 5 yellow squares out of 100. We can write this as 5%. This is the same as $\frac{5}{100}$, $\frac{1}{20}$ or 0·05.

All the squares added together – red, blue, green and yellow – represent 100%.
This is the same as $\frac{100}{100}$ or 1.

 Say Look carefully at the 100 square again.

Can you visualise each of the equivalent percentages, fractions and decimals mentioned? Point some of these out to a partner.

Look at this bar model. It shows equivalences between different percentages, fractions and decimals.

10% $\frac{1}{10}$ 0·1	10% $\frac{1}{10}$ 0·1	10% $\frac{1}{10}$ 0·1	10% $\frac{1}{10}$ 0·1	10% $\frac{1}{10}$ 0·1	10% $\frac{1}{10}$ 0·1	10% $\frac{1}{10}$ 0·1	10% $\frac{1}{10}$ 0·1	10% $\frac{1}{10}$ 0·1	10% $\frac{1}{10}$ 0·1

We can also see that this blue part represents $\frac{2}{10}$.

20% $\frac{1}{5}$ 0·2	20% $\frac{1}{5}$ 0·2	20% $\frac{1}{5}$ 0·2	20% $\frac{1}{5}$ 0·2	20% $\frac{1}{5}$ 0·2

25% $\frac{1}{4}$ 0·25	25% $\frac{1}{4}$ 0·25	25% $\frac{1}{4}$ 0·25	25% $\frac{1}{4}$ 0·25

We can also see that this orange part represents $\frac{5}{10}$.

50% $\frac{1}{2}$ 0·5	50% $\frac{1}{2}$ 0·5

Say Use the bar model above to convert these percentages into fractions and decimals.

| 30% | 40% | 60% | 70% | 75% | 80% | 90% |

We can also use number lines to represent equivalent percentages, fractions and decimals.

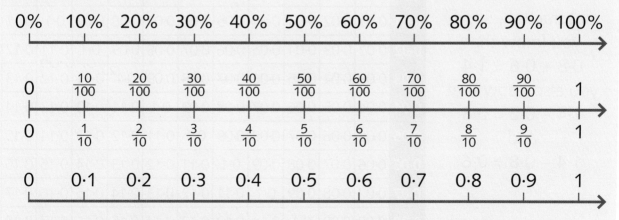

Look at the number lines above.

What are the percentage and decimal equivalences for each of these fractions?

$\frac{1}{5}$ $\frac{2}{5}$ $\frac{3}{5}$ $\frac{4}{5}$

Year 5 Number facts

Tenths and hundredths addition and subtraction facts

If you know that 8 + 6 = 14, you can use this to work out facts such as:

0·8 + 0·6 = 1·4

and

0·08 + 0·06 = 0·14

Addition can be done in any order. So,

0·8 + 0·6 = 1·4

and

0·6 + 0·8 = 1·4

Addition is the inverse of subtraction. So, if you know that

0·8 + 0·6 = 1·4

you also know that

1·4 − 0·6 = 0·8

and

1·4 − 0·8 = 0·6

+	0	0·1	0·2	0·3	0·4	0·5	0·6	0·7	0·8	0·9	1
0	0	0·1	0·2	0·3	0·4	0·5	0·6	0·7	0·8	0·9	1
0·1	0·1	0·2	0·3	0·4	0·5	0·6	0·7	0·8	0·9	1	1·1
0·2	0·2	0·3	0·4	0·5	0·6	0·7	0·8	0·9	1	1·1	1·2
0·3	0·3	0·4	0·5	0·6	0·7	0·8	0·9	1	1·1	1·2	1·3
0·4	0·4	0·5	0·6	0·7	0·8	0·9	1	1·1	1·2	1·3	1·4
0·5	0·5	0·6	0·7	0·8	0·9	1	1·1	1·2	1·3	1·4	1·5
0·6	0·6	0·7	0·8	0·9	1	1·1	1·2	1·3	1·4	1·5	1·6
0·7	0·7	0·8	0·9	1	1·1	1·2	1·3	1·4	1·5	1·6	1·7
0·8	0·8	0·9	1	1·1	1·2	1·3	1·4	1·5	1·6	1·7	1·8
0·9	0·9	1	1·1	1·2	1·3	1·4	1·5	1·6	1·7	1·8	1·9
1	1	1·1	1·2	1·3	1·4	1·5	1·6	1·7	1·8	1·9	2

+	0	0·01	0·02	0·03	0·04	0·05	0·06	0·07	0·08	0·09	0·1
0	0	0·01	0·02	0·03	0·04	0·05	0·06	0·07	0·08	0·09	0·1
0·01	0·01	0·02	0·03	0·04	0·05	0·06	0·07	0·08	0·09	0·1	0·11
0·02	0·02	0·03	0·04	0·05	0·06	0·07	0·08	0·09	0·1	0·11	0·12
0·03	0·03	0·04	0·05	0·06	0·07	0·08	0·09	0·1	0·11	0·12	0·13
0·04	0·04	0·05	0·06	0·07	0·08	0·09	0·1	0·11	0·12	0·13	0·14
0·05	0·05	0·06	0·07	0·08	0·09	0·1	0·11	0·12	0·13	0·14	0·15
0·06	0·06	0·07	0·08	0·09	0·1	0·11	0·12	0·13	0·14	0·15	0·16
0·07	0·07	0·08	0·09	0·1	0·11	0·12	0·13	0·14	0·15	0·16	0·17
0·08	0·08	0·09	0·1	0·11	0·12	0·13	0·14	0·15	0·16	0·17	0·18
0·09	0·09	0·1	0·11	0·12	0·13	0·14	0·15	0·16	0·17	0·18	0·19
0·1	0·1	0·11	0·12	0·13	0·14	0·15	0·16	0·17	0·18	0·19	0·2

Multiplication and division facts

Multiplication can be done in any order.

So, 3 × 4 = 12 and
4 × 3 = 12

Multiplication is the inverse of division.

So, if you know that 3 × 4 = 12 you also know that

12 ÷ 4 = 3 and 12 ÷ 3 = 4

×	1	2	3	4	5	6	7	8	9	10	11	12
1	1	2	3	4	5	6	7	8	9	10	11	12
2	2	4	6	8	10	12	14	16	18	20	22	24
3	3	6	9	12	15	18	21	24	27	30	33	36
4	4	8	12	16	20	24	28	32	36	40	44	48
5	5	10	15	20	25	30	35	40	45	50	55	60
6	6	12	18	24	30	36	42	48	54	60	66	72
7	7	14	21	28	35	42	49	56	63	70	77	84
8	8	16	24	32	40	48	56	64	72	80	88	96
9	9	18	27	36	45	54	63	72	81	90	99	108
10	10	20	30	40	50	60	70	80	90	100	110	120
11	11	22	33	44	55	66	77	88	99	110	121	132
12	12	24	36	48	60	72	84	96	108	120	132	144

Tenths and hundredths multiplication and division facts

If you know that 3 × 4 = 12, you can use this to work out facts such as:

0·3 × 4 = 1·2 and 0·03 × 4 = 0·12

Multiplication is the inverse of division. So, if you know that 0·3 × 4 = 1·2 you also know that

1·2 ÷ 4 = 0·3 and 0·12 ÷ 4 = 0·03

×	0·1	0·2	0·3	0·4	0·5	0·6	0·7	0·8	0·9	1	1·1	1·2
1	0·1	0·2	0·3	0·4	0·5	0·6	0·7	0·8	0·9	1	1·1	1·2
2	0·2	0·4	0·6	0·8	1	1·2	1·4	1·6	1·8	2	2·2	2·4
3	0·3	0·6	0·9	1·2	1·5	1·8	2·1	2·4	2·7	3	3·3	3·6
4	0·4	0·8	1·2	1·6	2	2·4	2·8	3·2	3·6	4	4·4	4·8
5	0·5	1	1·5	2	2·5	3	3·5	4	4·5	5	5·5	6
6	0·6	1·2	1·8	2·4	3	3·6	4·2	4·8	5·4	6	6·6	7·2
7	0·7	1·4	2·1	2·8	3·5	4·2	4·9	5·6	6·3	7	7·7	8·4
8	0·8	1·6	2·4	3·2	4	4·8	5·6	6·4	7·2	8	8·8	9·6
9	0·9	1·8	2·7	3·6	4·5	5·4	6·3	7·2	8·1	9	9·9	10·8
10	1	2	3	4	5	6	7	8	9	10	11	12
11	1·1	2·2	3·3	4·4	5·5	6·6	7·7	8·8	9·9	11	12·1	13·2
12	1·2	2·4	3·6	4·8	6	7·2	8·4	9·6	10·8	12	13·2	14·4

×	0·01	0·02	0·03	0·04	0·05	0·06	0·07	0·08	0·09	0·1	0·11	0·12
1	0·01	0·02	0·03	0·04	0·05	0·06	0·07	0·08	0·09	0·1	0·11	0·12
2	0·02	0·04	0·06	0·08	0·1	0·12	0·14	0·16	0·18	0·2	0·22	0·24
3	0·03	0·06	0·09	0·12	0·15	0·18	0·21	0·24	0·27	0·3	0·33	0·36
4	0·04	0·08	0·12	0·16	0·2	0·24	0·28	0·32	0·36	0·4	0·44	0·48
5	0·05	0·1	0·15	0·2	0·25	0·3	0·35	0·4	0·45	0·5	0·55	0·6
6	0·06	0·12	0·18	0·24	0·3	0·36	0·42	0·48	0·54	0·6	0·66	0·72
7	0·07	0·14	0·21	0·28	0·35	0·42	0·49	0·56	0·63	0·7	0·77	0·84
8	0·08	0·16	0·24	0·32	0·4	0·48	0·56	0·64	0·72	0·8	0·88	0·96
9	0·09	0·18	0·27	0·36	0·45	0·54	0·63	0·72	0·81	0·9	0·99	1·08
10	0·1	0·2	0·3	0·4	0·5	0·6	0·7	0·8	0·9	1	1·1	1·2
11	0·11	0·22	0·33	0·44	0·55	0·66	0·77	0·88	0·99	1·1	1·21	1·32
12	0·12	0·24	0·36	0·48	0·6	0·72	0·84	0·96	1·08	1·2	1·32	1·44